Praise for *Raising a Self-Reliant Child*

"Dr. Alanna Levine's book on helping parents back off from the Black Hawk approach to parenting is not only timely but also crucial for our children's emotional health and well-being. Reports just released from UCLA show the incoming crop of freshmen to have record high levels of stress and the all-time lowest mental health in twenty-five years. Our ultimate parenting goal is to raise independent, well-adjusted kids who can someday live without us. Dr. Levine's book will give parents the knowledge and tools to do so."

—MICHELE BORBA, educational psychologist, author of *The Big Book of Parenting Solutions*, *TODAY* show contributor

"Alanna Levine has done a great service to parents everywhere with this authoritative guide to raising children who can grow up to be self-sufficient adults. Far from the extremes of the Tiger Mother or the helicopter parent is the empowering parent—one who understands that fostering a 'can-do' spirit in young children rather than doing everything for them will result in happier children and happier families. Parenting according to the principles in *Raising a Self-Reliant Child* will give childhood back to children, and frazzled parents will find they have more time and a better relationship with their children."

—DR. TANYA REMER ALMANN, pediatrician, author of *Mommy Calls*, American Academy of Pediatrics spokesperson

"Dr. Alanna finds a way to make the everyday challenges of raising young children seem logical and manageable. Drawing on her experience as a doctor and a mother, she provides relatable and real information and guidance. This is a great resource for parents and grandparents!"

—DR. JENNIFER ASHTON, women's health expert,
author of *The Body Scoop for Girls*

"Dr. Levine's book, *Raising a Self-Reliant Child*, is exactly what today's parents need. Instead of raising your child to be your best friend, following Dr. Alanna's approach will help you take a fresh look at how to handle the most common challenges of early childhood. From bedtime battles and basic discipline to troubles with toilet training, this book will ultimately help you raise a more caring, independent, and self-confident child."

—DR. LAURA A. JANA, pediatrician, author of
Heading Home with Your Newborn: From Birth to Reality,
American Academy of Pediatrics spokesperson

Raising a
Self-Reliant
Child

Raising a Self-Reliant Child

A Back-to-Basics Parenting Plan
from Birth to Age 6

Dr. Alanna Levine

TEN SPEED PRESS
Berkeley

Ten Speed Press and the Ten Speed Press colophon are registered
trademarks of Random House, Inc.

Library of Congress Cataloging-in-Publication Data
Levine, Alanna, 1973-
  Raising a self-reliant child : a back-to-basics parenting plan from
birth to age 6 / Alanna Levine.
      p. cm.
  Includes bibliographical references and index.
1. Parenting. 2. Child rearing. 3. Self-reliance in children. I. Title.
  HQ755.8.L4887 2013
  649'.1—dc23

                            2012045631

Trade Paperback ISBN: 978-1-60774-350-7
eBook ISBN: 978-1-60774-351-4

Printed in the United States of America

Design by Chloe Rawlins
Front cover photograph by Image Source

10 9 8 7 6 5 4 3 2

First Edition

Contents

Acknowledgments

As a first-time author, I have truly engaged the help of a village of people to produce this finished product. It all began with Marta Tracy. This book would not be on the shelves today without her belief in me and her tireless effort and introductions to all of the "right people." Among many other important meetings, she is directly responsible for introducing me to my literary agent, Frederica Friedman.

Fredi understood my concept immediately, and from that very first encounter, she became a true champion for the book. She was involved in every step of the process from the proposal right through the final version of the manuscript.

I thank my editor, Sara Golski from Ten Speed Press, for her gentle manner and patience as I embarked on this new journey. And a big thank you to Julie Bennett, also at Ten Speed Press, for understanding the need for this book to be written.

Many thanks to Elisa Petrini who has guided me through the author process and has also helped turn my ideas into grammatically correct sentences.

I have been fortunate enough to have a team of experts to advise me. I am forever grateful to my media agent, Mark Turner of Abrams Artists, who is available 24-7 for anything I need. My attorney, Tom Distler, is always behind me every step of the way.

To the incredible doctors and staff at Orangetown Pediatric Associates, I express my sincere thanks for always being there to support me. I think of all of you not just as coworkers but as good friends.

My pediatric colleagues across the country have also been integral to the writing process. Dr. Tanya Remer Altmann has been a great friend and mentor to me. She read drafts on numerous occasions and offered her insight on how to turn a book concept into a reality. Dr. Laura Jana has gone over the manuscript with a fine-tooth comb, despite her out-of-control crazy schedule. Dr. Wendy Sue Swanson always put the world in perspective for me, which is something a full-time working mother who wants to write a book in her spare time desperately needs. Dr. Ari Brown and Dr. Jennifer Shu are always on call to answer any of my pediatric and author questions. I feel so fortunate to be surrounded by such a smart, energetic, and talented group of pediatricians and friends.

To my patients and their parents, who have served as the true backbone to this book, I offer a very special thank you. It's your stories and experiences that shaped the ideas for the book and many of the parenting strategies I use with my own children. I thank you very much for sharing them with me.

To my parents, parents-in-law, sisters, and beloved grandparents, I hope you know how supported I have always felt by you. There is no way I would have gone to medical school, completed a residency, had the courage to stand in front of a TV camera, and now be publishing a book if I hadn't had your relentless support. You celebrate each and every achievement right there along side of me, and I am eternally thankful and grateful for having the best family possible.

Jamie, my dear husband, has stuck right beside me for the past twenty-two years. He moved to Boston for graduate school, to Israel for medical school, and then still stood by me through three years of residency. And just when we thought life would become less complicated, I decided to broaden the reach of my pediatric practice and write medical articles, appear on TV, and now write a book! I thank you for being my rock, my adoring husband, and the best father to our children ever.

And to my children, Sophie and Charlie, I am so proud of you each and every day. You are the two most competent children I know, and your dedication and determination to achieve anything you desire is incredible to witness. I thank you for all that you have taught me about parenting. I love you so much!

The Self-Reliant Child: Instilling Independence from the Start

I see them everywhere: the exhausted, hollow-eyed zombie parents of children who never sleep; the sherpa parents, groaning under backpacks and diaper bags with kids hanging on each arm; the guard dog parents, catching children in midtumble; the food fighters, coaxing kids to eat anything that isn't white; the backseat parents, who finish or perfect whatever a child starts; the taxi parents, huddled in cars, poised to whisk children home from countless enrichment programs; the parents-at-arms, waging war over any real or potential slight. . . . The list goes on and on.

My heart goes out to all of these parents. I'm a pediatrician and a mother myself, so I can tell you from experience that your parenting life doesn't have to be that hard. By applying the lessons of this book, you can greatly benefit your child and, at the same time, improve the quality of your own life.

We all know what we want: children who are healthy, happy, creative, achievement focused, and likely to succeed in life, work, and love. We're ready to do whatever it takes to ensure such victories. But what it takes is the big question, and the answers parents hear often conflict.

Of course, there's no one "right way" to raise any given child. But, luckily, as I advise parents in my practice, there *is* a single, real-world principle—the Independence Principle—that comes as close as it gets to a universal approach to child rearing: *instill independence to promote self-reliance.*

Independence, or being allowed to develop your own powers, is the foundation of *self-reliance*, which is the ability to function on your own. For children to become self-reliant, we must give them the independence to find their own footing rather than hover, controlling their every thought and move. The Independence Principle, which we'll explore in this book through hands-on advice and parent-child stories, means empowering children, from birth onward, to discover and develop their own capacity for peaceful sleep, self-soothing, toilet training, healthy eating, impulse control, problem solving, and much more.

Allowing children to access their own powers requires that parents take a step back, curbing their own protective and indulgent interventions that, however natural, tend to impede kids' independent efforts at self-mastery. I'll offer guidelines to help parents recognize the difference between appropriate and smothering involvement, as well as techniques that can promote independence and self-reliance. By instilling these qualities in your children, you will pave their way to capable, confident, and self-sustaining young adulthood.

The Parent Trap

As parents today, we are swamped with advice and information. The blogosphere buzzes around the clock, chewing over new child-care fads that seem to crop up every month. The debates surrounding these fads are downright fierce, and the mommy boards are quick to scold parents who venture to stray from the latest accepted wisdom.

One type of parent most ridiculed today is the "helicopter parent," who coddles her kids and micromanages their every move. This parenting style may be rooted in 1970s attachment theories, later revived by experts like pediatrician William Sears. Dr. Sears has long urged parents to practice the "seven B's," which include, among others, baby wearing, birth bonding, and bedding (bed sharing), and to respond instantly to crying infants. This goal was, and continues to be, a noble one: to bond closely with infants to deepen their emotional security. And, let's face it, the concept is appealing. What could be more delicious than to snuggle with a little baby?

The trouble is that, for many parents, the bonding has no "off" switch, and they struggle with the seventh "B," which stands for balance. We're seeing the results today in a generation of young adults who seem destined to remain children.

Helicopter parents insulate kids from every possible discomfort. On a parenting blog, a fourth-grade principal complained of a mother disrupting lunch to bring her son extra ketchup;

another described a parent swooping in with her daughter's forgotten necklace. Some schools have had to establish a "no rescue" rule specifically to fend off parents dropping by to deliver last night's homework. Think about it: If parents always save the day, how can kids grow up? How can they learn accountability or gain the resilience to cope with disappointments bigger than a missing necklace?

With parents running their lives, some kids grow paralyzed with indecision. I've heard stories of college freshman texting their parents to ask what to eat for dinner. They've never had to think for themselves. And some of these parents don't even check their controls at the workplace door. When Michigan State University polled seven hundred firms, it found that nearly a third had received resumes submitted not by job-seeking grads but by their parents, sometimes without the job-seekers' knowledge; a quarter had fielded calls from parents pleading that children be hired; and at twenty-eight companies, parents had actually tried to sit in on their kids' job interviews.[1]

Can you imagine? It's hard not to laugh in horror at such over-the-top behavior, except for the fact that it's really not funny. Still, many parents can't resist the temptation to do it all—and to do it right—for their kids.

Clearly, a shift was needed. It emerged in a polar opposite style, promoted by Lenore Skenazy, called "free-range parenting." A New York journalist, Skenazy was reviled as "the worst mom in America" when she wrote an article published in the *New York Sun* in 2008 about letting her son ride the subway alone at the age of nine.[2] In the book that rose from that showdown, *Free-Range Kids: Giving Our Children the Freedom We Had Without Going Nuts with Worry*, Skenazy cites statistics showing that, despite our misperceptions, the world is actually safer now and is less crime-ridden than in supposedly idyllic decades past.[3] She describes how exhilarated her son was at his grownup journey. Even so, the mere image of a child alone underground in the dark and shadowy subway, out of cell phone range, is bloodcurdling for many parents.

Skenazy's theory, however, has gained some traction in the media. She writes frequently on free-range parenting and is the host of the TLC reality show *World's Worst Mom*.

On the other end of the spectrum is an equally controversial figure, the Tiger Mother, Amy Chua, who frowns on indulgence in favor of coercing high achievement from children. Her goals, described in her 2011 book, *Battle Hymn of the Tiger Mother*, fit perfectly with the aspirations of many high-achieving middle-class parents who marvel at the seeming superiority of Asian students.

What's the secret to raising such high-achieving kids? As Chua wrote in the *Wall Street Journal*, "Chinese parents believe that they know what is best for their children and therefore override all of their children's own desires and preferences. That's why Chinese daughters can't have boyfriends in high school and why Chinese kids can't go to sleepaway camp. It's also why no Chinese kid would ever dare say to their mother, 'I got a part in the school play.' God help any Chinese kid who tried that one."

Chua, who is Chinese, points out that other groups— "I know some Korean, Indian, Jamaican, Irish, and Ghanian parents who qualify too"—share the belief that academics (and maybe music) should be paramount, and if children don't excel, "parents are not doing their job." She adds that "Chinese parents can get away with things that would seem unimaginable . . . to Westerners. . . . Western parents are concerned about their children's psyches. . . . Chinese parents assume strength, not fragility."[4]

Of course, many in the blogosphere roundly denounced the Tiger Mother as abusive. Her philosophy spawned a virtual zoo of reactions, some tongue in cheek, including the Panda Father (favoring cuddling and chaos) and the Koala Mother (so all-natural as to advocate breast-milk popsicles to ease teething).[5]

And then there's Pamela Druckerman, the "French moms have got it right" author of the 2012 book *Bringing Up Bébé*, describing the child-rearing norms she observed while living in France. She contends that, in France, *bébés* sleep through the night within a month or two of birth, and toddlers not only eat calmly in restaurants but gobble broccoli and leeks like Sugar Pops.[6] Of course, mommy-board objections flared like wildfire—that French society is repressive, and so on—but not before stoking the insecurities of plenty of American parents.

Whew! These are just a handful of the parenting styles around today. Is it any wonder that parents are confused and so many ask, "What are we doing wrong? Should we be French, tiger, free-range, or attachment parents?"

The Independence Principle

The answer is no. The Independence Principle is the antidote to such parenting fads. I apply it in my own home, and I've seen my patients' parents reap immediate benefits when they try it. They're amazed that, in just a couple of weeks, their babies sleep through the night; their toddlers nap without them stretched alongside; their school-age children dress themselves, make breakfast, do their homework, and even resolve disputes with little parental intervention. What's more, their kids take pride in these achievements, delighting in saying, "Look, I did it all by myself." What greater gift could you give your child than the joy of competence?

This book will explain the whys and, more importantly, the hows of instilling independence and self-reliance. The time to lay the groundwork for future accomplishment is right from the start, in the years from birth to age six, when children's brains are getting organized. Brain-based research supports this fact and also affirms the value of instilling independence and, ultimately, self-reliance in your child.

In the 2011 book *Welcome to Your Child's Brain*, neuroscientists Sandra Aamodt and Sam Wang review the latest research to create a fascinating portrait of the developing mind. In essence, many of our essential early learned tasks—facial and speech recognition, language acquisition, the ability to walk, and so on—are hard wired. They happen automatically as babies simply exist in their environment. Parental attention can help the process along, and I encourage parents to smile at their babies and talk to them in sweet voices, but it's amazing how much occurs without intervention.

For example, newborns quickly show a preference for their native language and can distinguish it from other sounds, like the barking of the family dog. This discrimination occurs because genes map out basic brain connections, and the roads are filled in when the child interacts with his environment.

While the brain, more than parents, governs the language-learning process, the more parents talk and respond to a baby, the richer his brain maps become. Parents don't impose language on a child but stimulate his development through verbal connection, which engages the brain's natural language mechanisms.

The same applies to sleep. We all have internal clocks, referred to as *circadian rhythms*. When cued by light and darkness, these internal clocks time the release of hormones (the body's messengers) that determine our cycles of hunger, fatigue, and alertness. In the womb, a baby's circadian rhythms are regulated by his mother's. But from birth, as any new parent can attest, that clock goes seemingly haywire and days and nights get confused. Newborns sleep up to sixteen hours per day, but, initially, seem to be awake more at night than during the day.

By around three months old, the child's brain is primed for regulation, though not quite ready to embrace the night-and-day cycle. That's when parents can make a difference. As with language, they can't impose sleep, but if they're alert to the onset of drowsiness, they can capitalize on the brain's natural sleep mechanism by quickly putting the child to bed. Regular feeding times can make drowsy periods somewhat more predictable and help the infant brain sort out time patterns. Similarly, establishing a bedtime ritual can cue infants that each day is divided into intervals, filling in another brain map.[7]

The key is neither the Tiger Parent's coercion nor the strict controls and schedules that Druckerman credits with civilizing French babies. As Aamodt and Wang wrote in the *New York Times*, "Fortunately for American parents, psychologists find that children can learn self-control without externally imposed pressure. . . . The key is to harness the child's own drives for play, social interaction, and other rewards. Enjoyable activities elicit dopamine release to enhance learning, while reducing the secretion of stress hormones, which can impede learning and increase anxiety, sometimes for years."[8]

Putting the Independence Principle into Practice

These findings are a valuable backdrop for the ideas and techniques I'll be describing in this book. Since Aamodt and Wang are brain researchers, their notion of creating order in the mind through self-control makes sense. But as a pediatrician, I am committed to translating their fascinating scientific findings into everyday parenting techniques. I like to think in terms of the freedom and creativity born of competence, which is best achieved through *active*, rather than passive, learning.

To achieve competence, children need to *actively* build on lessons learned—in the basics like language and sleeping and also in play, friendship, conflict resolution, academics, ambition, and the many other arenas of our children's full and complicated lives. Parents can be present as guides, but it's the children who should do the work, make the mistakes, and learn from them. Isn't the very essence of growing up becoming increasingly self-sufficient and competent? Proficiency develops only if we grant children the space to achieve on their own. It is our ultimate job as parents to give our children wings so *they* can fly. That's why the Independence Principle is fundamental to parenting.

One Principle Fits All?

Because all our brains develop along the same kinds of circuits, the Independence Principle is universal. But that doesn't mean that it is one-size-fits-all. The degree of independence a child can and should handle—and when—is highly individual. You'll want to be attuned to your child, to her temperament, anxieties, and surroundings when you first start to foster or progress through independence. Proceed with compassion and prudence. This book will show you how, step by step, whether you're beginning in infancy or trying to push the "reset" button on behaviors that have gotten out of hand with your toddler or school-age child.

Independence in Action

Consider this epiphany that Nancy, the mother of a patient, told me that she'd experienced with her four-year-old at school.

> Josie was super-whiny when I went to pick her up. She wanted a snack in the car. She didn't want to go home yet. And she definitely didn't want to put on her jacket: "I hate it. It's too hot!"
>
> "But it's snowing outside. You'll freeze," I said. "Come on, you have to wear it."
>
> I stood there holding up the jacket for a few minutes while Josie danced around, ignoring me. "Come on, come on," I kept saying. Finally I got tired of the drama, and besides, I had to get home. It had been a long day, and I had dinner to figure out.
>
> I grabbed Josie and tried to wrestle her arms into the jacket, while she kept wriggling and yelling, "NO! NO!"

"Fine, you win," I said, in exasperation. Shoving the jacket into my bag, I made her step into her boots. That worked. But when I put on her hat, she tore it off and threw it on the floor. I would have lost it then, but other mothers were looking on, either smiling with recognition or glaring like I was an idiot. How embarrassing.

When we reached the door and opened it, the air rushing in was arctic. I pulled out Josie's jacket and made another try. "Come on, honey. See how cold it is? Let's put on your coat."

"NOOO!"

So we headed out to the car, with the jacket under my arm and Josie in just a sweater. Thank goodness, her defiance lasted for only a couple yards. Then she protested, "Mommy, I'm cold!"

"Okay," is all I said—not, "I told you so." I didn't want to rub it in.

Taking the jacket, Josie actually put her own arms in the sleeves. She even pulled up her hood. That was major.

Josie just had to learn for herself that she'd be cold without a jacket. It was like a lightbulb went on: cause and effect, action and consequence. That one simple experience taught her—and me—so much more than any number of lectures and power struggles.

Nancy's story highlights the tremendous power of natural consequences and active learning while teaching Josie a valuable lesson. Of course, no responsible parent would prefer to let a child go out in the snow without a coat. But to four-year-old Josie, it was important to exert control by refusing to wear the jacket; she didn't have the foresight to worry about being cold. The stakes were low enough—just a few chilly minutes—for Nancy to let her suffer the consequences of her insistence.

And, as Nancy points out, that discomfort was far more effective at getting Josie to bundle up than any line of reasoning or even physical coercion.

Obviously, no parent should ever expose a child to risk of harm. But when the peril is this minimal, parents can and should give up control, allowing children to make independent decisions to let them experience the consequences.

As parents, we encounter situations like Nancy's all the time. But we tend to focus on our own aggravation—*another fight with Josie!*—rather than recognize that these are "teachable moments" (much more is gained through the lesson of being cold than the battle over the jacket). As a result, our reactions are often wildly inconsistent (more on consistency later). If Nancy had felt less rushed, she might have waited for Josie to get tired of resisting, captured her, and put on the coat. That would have made the showdown a game, likely to be replayed in the future. Had her day been more stressful, Nancy might have flown off the handle and forced her daughter to get dressed. That probably would have precipitated a tantrum and left Nancy feeling like a monster.

Both scenarios would have been a waste of time and emotional energy. Worse, they would have cost Josie the chance to make her own decision, even if she made the wrong choice, and learn. And they would have cost Nancy the recognition that engaging in a power struggle is not always the most effective way to handle a child.

Balancing Control and Independence

Control is a challenging issue for parents today, for lots of reasons. First of all, this generation of parents is having fewer children— an average of 1.3 per family, versus 2.4 in 1970—and we want to ensure that each of them has a childhood that's as ideal as we can make it. We're also having children later in life—the average age of today's first-time mother is a little over twenty-five, versus twenty-one in 1970—so we often have more resources to invest in their happiness.[9]

As a generation, we are very dedicated parents. Sure, today more of us work (55 percent of first-time moms were back on the job within six months of giving birth, compared to 14 percent in 1960).[10] But as recently as 1995, American mothers spent about twelve hours per week on child care. By 2007, that average had risen to 21.2 hours for college-educated women and 15.9 hours for those with less education. In the same period, the time college-educated fathers spent with kids more than doubled, to 9.6 hours a week, and nearly doubled for other men, from 3.7 to 6.8 hours per week.[11]

What does this blast of statistics tell us? Among other things, that we want (and are expected) to be engaged more actively with our kids than was common in the recent past. It's not that we love our children more than our parents loved us but that now we're socialized to care for kids differently.

Look at how we regulate child safety—with video baby monitors, gates at the bottom and top of stairs, plugs in every outlet, and so on. While I certainly used some of this new technology with my own children, I also recognize that it reinforces the idea that children are fragile. It's natural that we want to protect them, but sometimes we go a little too far.

Another way that our lives have changed in the last few decades is that we are inescapably connected to one another. The buzz of constant communication has sped up the pace of life. Thanks to cell phones, texts, and email, we've grown conditioned always to be "on-demand," on duty and available. We're so on call for bosses, colleagues, relatives, and friends that it would be strange if we weren't as hyperresponsive to our children, reacting in ways that may limit their beneficial interactions with the world.

Even the most conscientious parents are vulnerable to these influences, as is illustrated in the following anecdote about a multitasking mom I met who was trying to tackle child care, grocery shopping, and work all at once.

> At the grocery store, I ran into Joanne, a mother with whom I occasionally chatted when I saw her at school functions. I knew she was an interior designer, so I wasn't surprised that she was glued to her cell phone, talking about colors. I smiled, and she stopped her grocery cart.
>
> In the cart was her younger son, who was close to three. He had a pacifier in his mouth. "Hi, there," I greeted him. "I'm Alanna. What's your name?"
>
> Before he could answer, Joanne broke from her call. "This is Lewis," she told me.
>
> "Hello, Lewis."
>
> He was clutching a box of animal crackers. He thrust it toward me, and I glanced at Joanne. She nodded, acknowledging that I should open it.

I lifted the cardboard seal and undid the waxy liner. As soon as I gave him back the box, Joanne stuck her hand inside. She pulled out a few of the crackers and gave them to her son.

"Which animals do you have?" I asked Lewis.

Again, Joanne stopped talking to her client. "That's a lion and a seal," she said. "Right? He likes lions."

Lewis yanked out the pacifier and shoved the crackers in his mouth.

At his age, Lewis could certainly tell me his own name. (I knew from our previous chats that he had no special language or developmental challenges.) At nearly three years of age, he should certainly have been able to open the box himself and pick out some animal crackers. The lion was easy to identify, especially for a boy who liked lions (even if the seal cracker was pretty much a blob).

But this was a child who couldn't get a word in edgewise. He didn't have to answer because Joanne did all the talking. As a further deterrent to interacting, his mouth was stuffed with a pacifier, as if he were two years younger. (I'll have more to say about pacifiers in chapter 2.) And it usually takes more than a lightly sealed box to keep a three-year-old away from snacks. Lewis hadn't tried to open the box but was waiting for an adult to do it. He was accustomed to having a very on-demand parent in Joanne, who had no idea that her hyperresponsiveness was actually infantilizing.

I'm telling this story not to criticize, but rather because Joanne's actions are so common. First of all, she was multitasking—hey, don't we all?—doing business on the phone while grocery shopping with her son. Sure, clients can be impatient. And yes, more than a few of us know the feeling of needing to be on call, day and night—I am a doctor, after all. But what's the message that Joanne-like behavior gives young children like Lewis? In addition to giving him the clear sense that no initiative whatsoever is needed on his part, it conveys all too loudly and clearly that if something seems difficult, have someone else do it for you. It also implies that everything has to be done right now, even if it pulls your mind in a million different directions—that focusing and living in the present are not important. It pays to be conscious of how often we model this not-so-healthy behavior for our children.

However, the big issue here, for our purposes, is the way Lewis was limited by Joanna's actions. It's easy to see how Joanne got in the habit of answering for her son. Children starting to talk are often unintelligible to anyone but their parents. Rather than watch them struggle to get the words out, many parents play translator. They take the quicker route of filling in the blanks. But by repeatedly filling in all of these typical blanks of childhood, they rob the child of the value of the interactions and the satisfaction of learning from them and ultimately being understood.

It's useful to also consider what is really gained by answering for the child—saving the questioner half a minute in our high-speed world? Did Joanne really think I cared which animals Lewis had? My aim was to engage him.

The same goes for opening the box and taking out the crackers. Why not let Lewis figure out how to do it and use his developing motor skills? Yes, it takes children longer to do what we accomplish in the blink of an eye. But it's not like Lewis had some more urgent task at hand. He didn't even get to choose which animals to eat because Joanne gave him the crackers. Where's the fun in that?

Perhaps he would have been too aggressive in opening the box and some of the contents would have spilled on the ground. So what? Lesson learned—be more careful next time. Perhaps he wouldn't have picked the lion that he really wanted and he would have had to figure out how to put it back and search out another one. It would have taken more time, but he would have been engaged in an active learning activity, which would have given Joanne more uninterrupted time on her phone call. I see that scenario as a win-win for both parent and child!

It's not easy to resist the urge to swoop in to rescue, to speak when we know the answer, and to watch our children make mistakes, but with practice, it becomes second nature. The result is competent, capable, successful, proud children, ready to take on the world.

CHAPTER 1

The Night Circus: Healthy Sleep Habits

Dina brought in her baby, Emily, for her six-month checkup. Emily seemed to be flourishing, grabbing my finger and kicking her legs, but Dina looked a little ragged around the edges. "How are you?" I asked. "How's Emily sleeping?"

"Not too well," she told me. "I'm back to work, and I thought that by now Emily would have gotten into a routine. But at night she still wakes up every couple of hours. I'm just beat."

"What do you do when she wakes up?" I asked.

"I nurse her. Sometimes I bring her into our bed. Or I rock her till she falls asleep in my arms, then I put her in her crib. But no matter where she falls asleep, she wakes up after just a few hours. Then the whole process starts over.

"What time do you put her to sleep?"

"Well, it depends. I miss her so much when I'm gone during the day. I get home around 6:30 and just grab a quick bite so I can play with her. I usually rock her to sleep—around 8 or 9, I guess—because she's crying. Then she wakes up at 11 or 12, again at 2 or 3, and she's up at 6. Aren't kids this age supposed to sleep thirteen hours? Emily naps a lot during the day, so I guess she gets enough sleep. But all I get is catnaps. Moms tell me that other kids her age sleep for five or more hours at a stretch. What a luxury! I'm so wrung out that I can hardly function. I am a walking zombie!"

There's no contest: sleep is the topic that stresses parents the most, both their children's and their own. There's nothing worse than feeling desperate for a good night's sleep and aching to comfort your child. An infant whose sleep cycle is out of whack disrupts the whole family. A toddler or preschooler who won't stay in bed can drive parents wild. And there's even more at stake when a child doesn't sleep than parental exhaustion and frustration.

As sleep expert Marc Weissbluth writes in his classic guide, *Healthy Sleep Habits, Happy Child*, "Sleep deficiency in childhood may harm neurological development. . . . I think it's possible that unhealthy sleep habits contribute to school-related problems such as attention deficit hyperactivity disorder (ADHD) and learning disabilities. I also suspect that chronically tired children become chronically tired adults who suffer in ways we can't measure: less resiliency, less ability to cope with life's stress, less curiosity, less empathy, less playfulness. The message here is simple: sleep is a powerful modifier of mood, behavior, performance, and personality."[1]

In an interview with the *Chicago Tribune*, Dr. Weissbluth elaborates on the significance of proper sleep and even compares it to the value of healthy eating and nutrition: "You would not starve your child by withholding food; try not to let your child get short on sleep." He also stresses the importance of nighttime or quality sleep over haphazard napping or so-called junk sleep. Dr. Weissbluth advocates that we should approach sleeping much like one might approach healthy eating. Junk food and junk sleep are okay once in a while, but not all of the time. Just as most parents read labels to try to give their children nutrient dense foods, parents should give the same attention to ensuring their children receive nourishing sleep.[2] (I'll discuss Dr. Weissbluth's highly effective sleep methods on page 24.)

Just think about how you feel when you don't get enough sleep. I know I feel irritable, short-tempered, and less able to regulate my emotions. I am more likely to get annoyed by things that don't ordinarily irritate me, and I also find it much harder to concentrate. Children who don't get enough sleep also have a hard time concentrating, are less coordinated, have increased aggression and hyperactivity, and are more at risk for obesity. Poor sleep interferes with learning and academic performance as well.[3] During childhood—such a critical time in development—we want to give our kids everything we can to maximize their chance to learn. We want them to feel happy and energetic to succeed at new challenges. Sleep is an important ingredient in the recipe for success!

These words are powerful motivators and parents can take comfort in the fact that far and away the vast majority of children, even those who seem dauntingly colicky and fussy, can and will learn to sleep peacefully. The key word here is *learn*. Learning to sleep without requiring doting, comforting parents is one of the first developmental tasks that a child must take on.

It might seem strange to think of sleep as something to learn—a skill like reading, writing, or walking. Yes, some parents are blessed with perfect sleepers right from birth, but many newborns don't instinctively know how to soothe themselves. Early on, they need us to calm them, and their developing nervous systems, by swaddling, cuddling, and rocking.

Older babies, however, have the capacity to self-soothe when given the opportunity to do so. We know that by the time they're a few months old, babies are ready to engage this important life skill—both by soothing themselves to sleep and back to sleep as they go through the normal cycles of light sleep and arousal throughout the night.

So the real question becomes how can babies discover this built-in capacity? Only through experience, by actually doing it and seeing how it works—by *active* learning. Sleeping is like walking, in this respect. When you stand up, you have to center yourself, training your muscles to keep your balance. In the same way, some babies who are a few months old must train their bodies to sleep.

Parents, with the most loving intentions, can stifle this natural impulse by making themselves essential to a baby's sleep process. Repeatedly rocking or nursing a child until he falls asleep and/or running in to pick him up at every whimper creates a dependency that is both unhealthy and may be hard to unravel later on. If every time a child topples, a parent picks him up and carries him, he will never learn the joy of getting somewhere on his own. If every time a child wakes up, a parent runs in to put him back to sleep, it will be unlikely that he will learn to fall asleep on his own.

A Canadian study of more than two thousand babies showed that children who had not learned to "consolidate" sleep—that is, to stay asleep for six straight hours on most nights—between the ages of five and seventeen months old were unlikely to do so at twenty-nine months. They had officially become what the researchers called "poor sleepers," unable to achieve the "quality sleep" that is so important, for the all reasons that Weissbluth details above.

What stops babies from learning to consolidate sleep? The chief cause is often parental attention, both at bedtime and during nighttime awakenings. To quote the researchers' own conclusion: "The present study lends support to the recommendation of putting children to bed while they are dozy but still awake so that they can develop appropriate sleep-onset associations. Similarly, in response to a nocturnal awakening, comforting children outside their beds (for example, feeding children, bringing children into the parents' beds, or rocking them outside their beds) is associated with poor sleep consolidation across early childhood, in contrast to comforting children in their own beds."[4]

In other words, you are not doing your child any favors by making a habit of snuggling him until he's fast asleep or taking him into your bed during the night. Instead, you're depriving him of the chance to learn the essential skill of sleeping on his own.

I explain to parents that infants, toddlers, and even older children (who, for whatever reason, have regressed) learn good sleep habits through independence. So, how you do give children this necessary independence? I'll outline below the methods of two top sleep authorities, Dr. Weissbluth and Dr. Richard Ferber, author of *Solve Your Child's Sleep Problems*, describing how each teaches parents to surrender a degree of control so as to better empower their children to sleep.

First-Year Follies

Newborns normally sleep in intervals of two to four hours, waking up to eat. By four months old, some babies, but not most, will sleep for five or six straight hours at night, with regular daytime naps. By some estimates, it's not until six months that 60 percent of babies sleep for a solid six to twelve hours and not until nine months that 80 percent do a regular all-night stretch.

That's why I reassured Dina, the sleep-deprived mother of my six-month-old patient, Emily, that nothing was inherently wrong—that her baby's sleep habits were more the rule than the exception. With a few adjustments, Dina's daughter would be sleeping five to six hours straight, just like her friends' babies. At six months old, Emily was the perfect age for Dina to help make this happen by instilling good sleep habits.

For the first few months of your baby's life, all the snuggling, nuzzling, and caressing you do go is a great aid to development, as it builds a sense of security and comfort. But according to Ferber, when it comes to sleeping, that comfort can be distracting as a child gets older.

Ferber's and Weissbluth's sleep methods—both successful—are grounded in independence, and we can analyze Dina's situation from both points of view. Of course, before embarking on any sleep-promoting program, you should check with your pediatrician. There may be special considerations, like failure to thrive or other health issues, that could affect your own child's sleep recommendations.

The Weissbluth Method

Dr. Weissbluth (father of four, distinguished pediatrician for nearly forty years, and founder of the Sleep Disorders Clinic at Chicago's Children's Memorial Hospital) urges parents to tune into their babies' sleep rhythms and establish strict naptimes and bedtimes. For babies Emily's age, he recommends a waking time of 7:00 a.m., followed by naps of at least an hour at 9:00 a.m. and between noon and 2:00 p.m., a briefer nap at 5:00 p.m., and bedtime around 7:00 p.m. Slightly older infants who skip the third nap may be ready for bed around 6:00 p.m. He cautions working parents against coming home and keeping their babies up to play, for fear of overstimulating them and causing them to miss their natural "sleep windows." If you put the child in bed during the window of opportunity, when she is awake but naturally drowsy (as shown by diminished alertness, eye rubbing, and similar signs), she will learn to drop off to sleep much more easily and independently. Failure to maintain fixed schedules, Weissbluth warns, will result in children who fight sleep or waken during the night because they are overtired.[5]

According to Weissbluth's theory, Dina was probably keeping her baby up too late, missing her sleep window. She was not enforcing a sufficiently strict nap schedule or practicing a regular calming routine before putting Emily to bed. (The calming ritual is a critical step, to be implemented before the child goes to bed but not after nighttime awakenings. The Sleep Rehearsal sidebar on page 26 offers some ideas for calming rituals.) Dina was unknowingly stimulating Emily too much before bedtime, and Emily was awakening often during the night because she was overtired from the too-long day.

According to Weissbluth, many babies can start "sleep training," as he calls it, when they're about six weeks old (or six weeks after the mother's due date, if they were born prematurely). Sleep training entails being in tune with your baby's need to sleep— even anticipating it, recognizing signs of drowsiness, and developing a bedtime routine. I agree with Weissbluth—it's best to start this from a young age. I think of it as a "respect" for your child's need to sleep. Initially, this can mean simply looking for cues of drowsiness, but as your child reaches four to six months of age, a schedule becomes increasingly important. The greatest challenge, however, typically comes when parents are confronted with their baby's crying. What do you do when you know your child is sleepy, but she just won't sleep? Weissbluth advocates (as do I) letting a child cry "to extinction," the technical term for becoming exhausted and all "cried out." At six months, the extinction period can be an hour at naptime and indefinite—as long as it takes for the baby to fall asleep—at night.[6] The good news is that many babies this age discover their own capacity for self-soothing within a week, if not sooner.

But for parents, the process can be agony. You have to ask yourself whether you can bear to resist a wailing child. You and your partner must be equally committed and prepared to be perfectly consistent. If you succumb to the burning urge to comfort your baby, all you'll be teaching is that crying hard and long enough is sure to bring parents running.

I tried this method with my own children, and it definitely works—but it is not easy. Be forewarned—you may feel cruel and guilty. Some parents stay glued to the baby monitor, to feel

The Sleep Rehearsal

Research shows and experts agree that a consistent calming ritual before you put your child to bed can ease him into sleep. You'll want apply the same practices most nights so your baby comes to see them as drowsiness triggers. A bedtime ritual can be very satisfying for parents too, a special time to relax with your baby.

Remember that this ritual is for putting a child to sleep. It is not an appropriate response to nighttime wakenings, when you want to minimize contact to avoid confusion.

Here are some ideas for different age groups.

- **Babies from Birth to Six Weeks Old.** Many babies fall asleep while nursing or drinking a bottle at this age. If this happens, simply and quietly transfer the baby to his sleeping environment. You don't have to wake him up first.

- **Babies from Six Weeks to Four Months Old.** Cuddling, singing (especially a favorite good-night song), and storytelling are all good ways to calm your baby down. Keep the sleep area dark. Nursing and rocking will help, of course, as long as your child doesn't fall sleep in your arms. You can play some soft music connected to the crying baby, while others seek the distraction of music or videos to muffle their anxiety. (It can be admittedly reassuring to peek in now and then to make sure the child is okay—I did—as long as she doesn't see you.) Many parents fear that this "abandonment" will be traumatic, with mental or physical consequences down the road. However, research hasn't shown that a few nights of crying have any lasting effects, while the potential risks of sleep deprivation, for both babies and parents, are well known.[7] If the extinction method feels

at low volume, if you like, or turn on a white-noise machine. Some parents like to slow dance with babies to the soft music. A warm bath, followed by a clean diaper and a gentle massage, can be a powerful sleep inducer—as well as a chance for either parent to soothe the child.

Try not to resort to desperate measures—like driving the baby around in the car or running the vacuum cleaner—so the child doesn't come to associate sleep with these sounds. The goal is to establish a nightly rhythm that will ease your child, let you watch for signs of drowsiness, and put him down awake to soothe himself.

- **Babies from Five to Twelve Months Old.** Keep practicing the strategies above, but you might want to add a verbal ritual, like walking the baby gently around the darkened room to say good night to objects or to the sun and moon. Stay positive, both verbally and nonverbally, reassuring the child that he will soon be fast asleep. Quash your own anxiety about his wakefulness because babies are highly attuned to their parents' distress. Finish with a bedtime story before putting your baby down to sleep.

too extreme for you, see the discussion below of Ferber's more graduated approach.

As babies get to be Emily's age, four to six months old, nighttime feedings generally subside or are limited to once or twice per night. If your child is still nursing multiple times during the night at six months, you may need to facilitate this process (after consulting your pediatrician) by reducing the number of feedings one at a time, a few days apart. This will likely lead to some crying and you can choose the extinction method above or the more gradual Ferber method described below. The strict scheduling Weissbluth advocates can be tough for parents, but respecting a child's sleep early on is important for longtime success. It may interfere with your plans for the day, but it will ultimately make your nights easier.

The Ferber Method

Many parents in my practice, including Dina, don't feel comfortable with Dr. Weissbluth's total extinction method (and Dr. Weissbluth does acknowledge some parents feel better with a more gradual approach), because they feel the need to check in with their baby during the crying process. For these parents, I recommend Ferber's strategy, which is also fairly strict but a little milder. Dr. Ferber is the director of the Center for Pediatric Sleep Disorders at Boston Children's Hospital and associate professor of neurology at Harvard. As one of the biggest names in sleep strategies, Dr. Ferber recommends building good "sleep associations," such as putting a baby to sleep in the same place he'll be should he awaken during the night (that is, not in your arms, rocking in a chair; not in your bed; not in front of the TV). If you don't put the baby to sleep in the same place, rather than learn to soothe himself, he may require the same cuddling, rocking, TV noise, and so on, to help him go back to sleep.[8]

Like Weissbluth, Ferber stresses the importance of a regular nap and night schedule (though he is less a proponent of early bedtimes). He also favors a consistent pre-sleep ritual, including cuddling and rocking, as long as the baby goes to bed drowsy but awake. But the big difference in his strategy is a practice called "progressive waiting," which gives parents the chance to connect, though not fully interact, with their babies. It keeps their attention focused on the clock, rather than on their child's distress, which can ease parents' anxiety. Ferber notes that the actual intervals that you wait before checking the baby are less important than keeping them consistent and progressively increasing the time. His recommendation is to start with intervals of three, five, and ten minutes.[9]

But the longer you wait at the outset, the more quickly your baby will grasp the process. So, here's what I recommend to parents of children aged four to six months and older.

Night 1

- Put your baby in the crib, then immediately leave the room. Your baby will probably stay awake and cry. Watch the clock and don't respond for five full minutes. If your baby is still crying, reenter the room to offer comfort like patting her or talking to her, but don't pick her up. Stay no longer than two or three minutes. It's important, Ferber says, not to sneak away if the baby is awake. Let her see you leave.

- Let ten minutes pass, and then go back to the baby. Repeat the comforting gestures, without picking your baby up, and again leave after two or three minutes.

- The next time, check your baby after fifteen minutes. If he's crying, then comfort him and, after two or three minutes, leave. Repeat the steps every fifteen minutes until he finally falls asleep.

Night 2

- Put your baby to bed awake but drowsy. Leave the room but hold off on your first check for ten full minutes. If needed, offer comfort and leave, just as on Night 1.

- On the next go-round, wait fifteen minutes before returning and repeating the steps.

- For round 3, let twenty minutes pass before checking in on your baby. Continue to visit him, comfort him, and leave at twenty-minute intervals while he remains awake.

Night 3

- Wait fifteen minutes before first checking on your baby and going through the ritual. Wait twenty minutes before round 2, and then twenty-five before your third return. Continue to check the baby every twenty-five minutes until he falls asleep.

Thereafter

- Each succeeding night, tack five minutes onto your first, second, and third visits. Most babies won't take more than a few days to grasp that, when you leave the room, they're supposed to fall asleep.

That's what happened for Dina. She told me:

We started the program on a three-day weekend so we'd have time to relax, if need be. The first night, Emily cried for ninety minutes straight. "I can't take this," I thought. Bill, my poor husband, had to spur me on.

I was filled with dread all Saturday. What if Emily cried for hours, while I had to keep waiting to check her? But that second night, she cried for forty-five minutes. Things were looking up. On Sunday night, she was down to twenty minutes—amazing. Then on Monday, she dropped off without a whimper and, incredibly, slept right through for six hours! Bill and I were overjoyed.

Of course, not everyone has Dina's fast track to success, but these methods have real power. Yes, there's plenty of debate on the mommy blogs and lots of criticism. ("Crying it out is like child abuse," one mother claimed.) But, as the Canadian study shows, learning to self-soothe is a critical skill for babies, and the best way to help a child sleep through the night is to engage this internal ability.[10] Staring at a mobile, a picture, or even his own hand can help a baby doze off and will teach him that he is capable of self-comforting.

There is no one right way to sleep-train a child and no shortage of strategies to try. One that I emphatically oppose is the bed sharing that attachment parenting advocates (see the

Co-Sleeping vs. Bed Sharing sidebar below). To reduce the risk of SIDS (sudden infant death syndrome), the safest place for a baby to sleep is in his own sleeping environment.

Families have been bed sharing since time began, but as Ferber points out, for most of those eons, they were lying on the ground, not on puffy mattresses with pillows and quilts—suffocation risks—and not enclosed by walls, where a baby's face might get trapped.[11] An American Academy of Pediatrics task force on SIDS states unequivocally that "several case studies of accidental suffocation or death from undetermined cause suggest that bed sharing is hazardous."[12]

Back on Track

So now you have a baby who has been sleeping through the night for a few months and suddenly she is waking up again—what do you do? It is common for parents who sleep-train their babies

Co-Sleeping vs. Bed Sharing

It's important to make the distinction between co-sleeping and bed sharing because sometimes the terms are used interchangeably, which can be confusing. *Co-sleeping* refers to having your child sleep in close proximity to you—in the same room—so you can see/hear/touch her. *Bed sharing* is a specific type of co-sleeping where the infant is on the same surface as the adult. The recommendation from the American Academy of Pediatrics is for room sharing without bed sharing for young babies, as there is evidence that room sharing, which allows you to keep tabs on the baby without the risks of bed sharing, reduces SIDS by as much as 50 percent.[13]

early on to see their work undone from time to time. A vacation can derail it, or a new developmental milestone can get in the way, as can illness or a new tooth. Don't panic! If you have already instilled good sleep habits, it will be easy to get back on track.

Babies change. They acquire new skills like rolling over and pulling up to stand in the crib and cannot return to their original position. Teething can also make some babies uncomfortable at night. So, you'll find from time to time that your baby's sleep lessons need refreshing. Sleep routines are like many other learned behaviors: they need reinforcement to take hold.

There are certain predictable times when you're more likely to need to restore good sleep habits. One of them occurs at around nine months, as the following story shows.

> David, Harry's father, was a violinist with the Philharmonic. His wife, Karen, had a corporate job, and since David was free in the daytime, he often came to my office with nine-month-old Harry.
>
> Harry seemed to be in great form, jabbering away. After the usual nine-month exam and questions about his movements ("Scooting around like crazy") and diet ("He loves picking up blueberries; he shoved a whole fistful of cereal into his mouth!), our conversation turned to Harry's sleep habits. "He's changed," David told me. "He really seems to miss us at night. I think he hates being all alone in his room.
>
> "Checking on him seems hopeless. When he sees us, he wants to play. We were doing sort of a Weissbluth thing, trying to ignore him, but it's hard. Then, the other night Harry really started howling, like something was terribly wrong. Of course, Karen rushed in, and there he was, standing in a corner of his crib. He'd pulled himself up and couldn't figure out how to get down!"

Harry's behavior was perfectly normal. Between six and nine months old, babies get very sociable. They start to communicate, in baby blabber, of course, but you can hear mimicked cadences and words like "dada" when they vocalize. Wired to interact, they love your company, so it's hard for them at the end of the day when playtime stops.

Safe Slumbers

We know that the risk of SIDS (sudden infant death syndrome, sometimes referred to as "crib death") is greatest between birth and six months, with the peak danger zone being two to three months old. While the cause of SIDS remains unknown, the risk of SIDS has greatly declined ever since the 1994 launch of the American Academy of Pediatrics' (AAP) national "Back to Sleep" campaign strongly advised parents to put babies to sleeps on their backs and *not* on their stomachs.[14]

Subsequent warnings have highlighted the hazards of soft mattresses, as well as extra bedding like pillows, top sheets, quilts, and fluffy blankets. Stuffed animals, sheepskins, and crib bumpers might look comforting to you, but they can pose a suffocation hazard to your child. Wedges, which some parents use to prop babies on their sides, are also not recommended. In short, *nothing should ever be placed in a crib but a firm, well-fitted mattress, a tight-fitted bottom sheet, and your baby.* Here are some guidelines for safe, sweet slumbers, along with additional tips on helping your baby to sleep through the night.

- **Newborn Bassinet or Crib.** For the first few months, have your newborn sleep in a bassinet or a small crib beside your bed. It's easy enough to take him out to nurse, and you'll be able to keep an eye on him.

They can also start to experience separation anxiety at this age. They are beginning to grasp the notion of *object permanence*, meaning that they know that things—including you—don't vanish when they're out of sight. So, when you disappear, they want you back. That's why they love peek-a-boo: the thrill of seeing someone vanish, then return. And that's why bedtime,

- **Room Temperature.** Keep the room airy and comfortably cool, not overheated.

- **Smoking.** Smoking in the household heightens the risk of SIDS (along with causing many other harmful effects).

- **Full-Size Crib.** Once your baby is moving around and starting to roll over, move your baby into a full-size crib, ideally in a separate, nearby room. It will be easier (and less frustrating for your baby) to teach him to sleep independently if he can't sense your presence or see you.

- **Crib Safety Standards.** Be sure to choose a crib that complies with the latest safety standards. As of this writing, the federal standards were most recently revised in June 2011.[15] Don't accept a used crib from a relative or friend that doesn't meet the newest federal guidelines, and make sure your baby's crib is properly assembled.

- **Sleeping Position.** Sometime between three to seven months old, a back-sleeping baby may roll over onto his stomach during the night. Don't panic. It's not necessary to keep running in and shifting him onto his back. Simply continue to put him to sleep on his back in his safe and otherwise empty crib. If he rolls over, you can let him sleep undisturbed.

when you're going to leave them alone for hours on end, becomes a new challenge.

Now is when the comforting bedtime ritual or "sleep rehearsal" becomes especially important. You can spend time readying your child for bed by singing, reading, and cuddling to reassure her. But keep the routine consistent—the same length of time every night, the same number of songs and stories— just as you would for younger babies—to signal that this is not playtime but sleep preparation.

Then, at the first sign of drowsiness, put your child in bed, tell her you love her, say good night, and leave the room.

If you've laid the groundwork, teaching your baby to soothe herself independently, it will be that much easier when you have to repeat those lessons. Yes, she'll probably cry. If she seems genuinely distressed, as Harry did, peek in to make sure that nothing is really wrong. If a child has begun to stand in her crib, you'll only make it a game if you immediately rush to the rescue. Rest assured, gravity will eventually help her down. It will only take a few tries before she discovers this on her own.

And she will have learned a significant lesson: that she has the capacity to stand and lower herself on her own. If you keep flying in to help her lie down, it will take her that much longer to understand her own powers. Why deprive her of making that breakthrough?

So I told David to stay strong and keep trying the Weissbluth method. I find that it works better than progressive waiting at this age, when the sight of parents often sparks a child's playfulness. It's frustrating for a child to see the people whose attention she craves and then be denied that attention. As I've said, a quick peek is okay, but it's usually better for your baby to believe that you're not there than that you are ignoring her.

Letting a nine-month-old cry "to extinction" is challenging, but luckily, the lesson can take hold quickly—usually in as few as three to five nights. Some parents try to distract themselves from the crying with a movie or soothing music. Sure enough, that's what happened with Harry. After four tries, he finally got settled and resumed sleeping through the night, peacefully . . . until the next milestone!

The Toddler Trials

The toddler years—roughly defined as extending from age one to three—are the glory days of children's independence. Think of all the skills that toddlers learn: how to walk, climb, scribble, throw a ball, stack blocks (and knock them down), talk a bit and understand a lot more, and even respond to what you say. It's a time of heady experimentation, when children love testing out their newfound powers.

They're also developing a new willfulness, a budding sense of independence that characteristically includes saying "no" all the time. Believe it or not, this is actually a positive development, as it shows that they're both mature and secure enough to try to stand up to adults. But it certainly can be frustrating, especially when sleep becomes the battleground. Hard as it is to resist a wailing baby, it can be even tougher to weather a toddler's pleas and wails. Often it's hard for parents to tell if anything's actually wrong. So I was glad that Lena and Jeff brought sixteen-month-old Evan in to see me. The pediatrician's office is the place to start when a child's behavior is troubling.

Lena and Jeff were upset. For months, Evan had been very good-natured and a good sleeper. "I guess that's why I'm two months pregnant," Lena joked. "All that peace and quiet at night. . . . But I forgot how tired you can feel in your first trimester."

Now Evan was balking at naptime and by bedtime was exhausted and cranky. "So he fights us," Jeff said. "Our bedtime ritual is pretty solid—a warm bath often helps. We finally manage to get him to sleep, but then he wakes up in the night howling, begging to be picked up. I cannot tell if he is mad or afraid of something."

"I feel almost too tired to cope," Lena said, "though Jeff's great about night duty. My mom says it might be Evan's ears or else his molars coming in."

"Does he seem asleep when he's howling, or fully awake?" I asked.

"Definitely awake," Jeff assured me. "He's furious that we keep him in his crib."

Lena agreed. "And when Evan wakes up, he wants me instead of Jeff. I am so tired and really need my sleep, especially now!"

Teething was certainly a possibility, but when I examined Evan's gums, I didn't see any new teeth erupting. He was cheerful, with no signs of a cold or an ear infection either. From the history Lena and Jeff described, Evan seemed to have a definite goal in mind—to be picked up and held—and by a certain person, Lena. I see this type of behavior very frequently in my practice during the toddler years. Parents describe children who were great sleepers during infancy, and as they enter into toddlerhood, they all of the sudden regress in their sleep habits.

I encourage parents to try not to let a toddler see how stressed and upset they are when he resists sleep. Negative attention is still attention, which is gratifying. If you express frustration, you'll just reinforce opposition by showing your child that he's found a new way to keep you crib-side and focused on him.

So stay calm and remember the goal: you are fostering independence and self-reliance. You have to foster these qualities because you can't sleep for him. You are placing the responsibility to sleep on the only person who can make it happen: your child. And by giving him that responsibility, you are setting him up for a lifetime of healthy sleep habits and the ability to return to sleep should he awaken—at any age!

Easing the Passage to Independent Sleep

Now is definitely not the time to throw in the towel and yield to your child's demands. But you can make a few adjustments that may ease a toddler's passage to independent sleep:

- **Reduce Number of Naps.** If getting to bed is a struggle and your child is still taking two naps a day, try cutting it down to one. As before, watch for signs of drowsiness and put him down to nap and also to bed awake.

- **Avoid Play Before Bed.** Don't give the child your best attention right before bedtime. Establish a play period before you make dinner or maybe right after dinner, then give him a short break before you initiate the sleep ritual. Keep the sleep ritual separate and consistent so it remains a trigger for drowsiness.

- **Anticipate Needs.** Add elements to the sleep ritual that anticipate his needs, like one cup of warm milk (provided you have time to brush his teeth afterward) or one drink of water. The goal here is to forestall requests that become a game, keeping you running back and forth to the kitchen and prolonging the sleep process.

- **Create a Peaceful Environment.** Try giving your child a nightlight or some low, calming background music. As toddlers, some kids start to become afraid of the dark. My own children loved lava lamps, which are fun to look at and sort of hypnotic. Peaceful classical music, played

Sleep Reset

These steps can help focus your toddler's sleep habits so she can begin or resume sleeping independently.

NIGHT 1

- In a darkened room, place a chair a few feet from your child's crib. (The farther away the better, but if you have to sit next to the crib on the first night, that's okay.)

- Do not pick up your child or take her out of the crib, even if she really fusses. If you have to pat her to comfort her or to get her to lie down, that's fine, but be brief—under a minute. Don't establish a pattern of extending back rubbing or massaging, which can make you a critical element of the sleep process. The goal is to empower her to soothe herself to sleep on her own.

- Speak to her reassuringly, telling her that you love her, that you're there, that it's now time for her to settle down and go to sleep. Keep repeating variations on this mantra. It's good to be boring! Stay in the chair until she dozes off. On subsequent nights, you'll want to work toward leaving the room while she is still awake but drowsy.

softly, or a white noise machine can also help a child stay focused on sleep.

- **Encourage Independent Play in Bed.** A child who is over a year old can have a few toys in his bed, like a board book or a stuffed animal (obviously, it must be child-safe, without button eyes or other detachable bits that might be swallowed). If he's not quite ready to sleep, he can amuse himself with toys in his bed, without you present.

NIGHT 2

- The next night, try to position the chair a few feet farther from the crib. You might be stuck in the same spot for a few nights, but don't revert and move the chair next to the crib. Repeat the same steps, and remember, don't pick her up.

NIGHT 3

- The following night, try moving the chair a few feet farther back. If your child gets frantic, don't push it. Keep some distance and just talk to her.

THEREAFTER

- Each succeeding night, try moving the chair a foot or two farther back, repeating the mantra. Your ultimate goal is to move the chair completely out of the room. This process can take a while, even a couple of weeks, depending on your child's age and determination. But stick with it. Keep your eyes on the prize: years of good, restorative sleep for your child and for the rest of your family.

- **Relinquish Some Control.** Give him an element of choice to satisfy his need for control: Which book do you want to take to bed? Which animal or toy? Which story do you want to hear? Which song? Expect him to test limits, pushing for one story to become three or two songs to become a symphony. Tell him in advance how many he gets to choose, then hold the line.

- **Express Confidence.** Be verbally reassuring and loving. A toddler understands many more words than he can say. So tell him how much you love him, that you know that he's going to sleep well and feel so good in the morning (or after his nap), and that you know he can do it.

After you've said goodnight, leave the room. Remember that you've done this before and how quickly your child got the message. The process may be a little harder because toddlers can really dig in their heels! But the foundation of good habits is there; your toddler just needs a refresher. And he will probably need a couple more refreshers down the road.

But what if your child, for whatever reason, doesn't have a consistent sleep regimen? What if a life event, like illness, separation, or even a long vacation, has thrown him off his sleep game? What if you've been bed sharing with your baby and now, in toddlerhood, need to get him out of your bed and onto the path to independence? The Sleep Reset sidebar on page 40 offers a strategy to help with that transition if you cannot just walk out of the room and listen to him being upset.

The Preschool Shuffle

The preschool years are an exciting period for both children and parents. This is the time when parents get to experience a child's unique personality—his likes, his dislikes, and his disposition. It's also a time when developmentally speaking, his skills are blossoming at lightning speed. As a child's determination grows, so does his ingenuity in accomplishing his goals. This can often create new challenges for parents, as evidenced by the following anecdote.

> My friend Susan and I had our first babies a few months apart. It was fun to compare notes when we were pregnant together and, when our children were born, to experience new motherhood side by side. Susan's son Lucas was a little older, so she would fill me in as he reached milestones that still lay ahead for my daughter. Even as a pediatrician, I found it fun to share our experiences together.
>
> One day Susan called me with big news. "I can't believe it. Last night Lucas woke me up with a big bellow. When I went to his room, I found him on the floor, looking shocked. He'd managed to climb out of his crib!
>
> "Now what am I supposed to do?"

Children are full of surprises. They're climbers and natural explorers. So the time may come, probably between eighteen and thirty-six months old, when your child will discover that he can escape from his crib.

One taste of freedom may not become a nightly habit, but, of course, you'll want to ensure his safety. Some cribs have settings that let you lower the mattress to make it harder for him to climb out—for a while. But it's time to embrace the inevitable: once your child can climb out of his crib, he's ready for a big-kid bed.

Just because it's time for a big-kid bed doesn't mean that your child is truly physically or emotionally prepared to make the transition. A good compromise is to simply take the mattress out of the crib and place it on the floor. Let the child sleep on the mattress until you feel certain that he won't roll off a higher bed and get hurt. Or get a bed with guard rails to keep your child secure until he adjusts to his big-kid status. Again, be sure that any bed you get meets the latest safety standards.[16]

You can make a little ceremony out of the bed transition. That's what Susan did, and in a few weeks, Lucas was safely installed in his own bed, getting ready for what I call, the "preschool shuffle."

Once your child is no longer enclosed in a crib, he is free to roam the house at will. Be sure to take the necessary precautions: secure the doors and windows with child-safe locks, and install gates at the top of the stairs, if needed.

It's most likely that your youngster will get out of bed, of his own volition, to make a beeline for your bedroom. That's when the "preschool shuffle" begins. Sometimes children migrate to their parents' room because of nightmares, but most often the reason is simple attraction to affection. Can you blame them? They now have physical independence, and they exercise it! Even so, think twice—make that three times—before taking your child into your bed. Do you really want to start all over again, reacclimating him to sleeping on his own?

I'm not suggesting that you should be hard-hearted and turn away a frightened child or a sick one. But keep in mind that one night in your bed will very likely be the first of many. As difficult as it is, I encourage parents to resist; it's better not to set foot on that slippery slope.

What you can do is walk—not carry—the child back to his room. Don't engage in a discussion or an argument. Say only, "You are a big boy. Big boys sleep in their own beds." Put him in his own bed and return to your own.

You may well have to repeat this "shuffle-back" process a number of times, even on the same night. Children can have a tenacity that outstrips that of most adults. If your child keeps popping up and appearing at your bedside, don't express exasperation—that's negative attention—but just keep walking him back to his own room. When he stays in his own bed, you can praise him, telling him how proud you are to see him growing up.

I firmly believe that your bedroom should be sacred, hallowed ground for you and the adult who sleeps beside you. Preserving that sanctity is not selfish; it's establishing a reasonable boundary for a child who is testing limits. It's reinforcing the lesson that he has the capacity to soothe himself, and helping him to access that power. Remember, you are setting him up for a lifetime of healthy sleep.

Feeling your own powers, having a sense of competence and of independent mastery, developing self-reliance: learning to sleep is where it all begins.

The Night Circus Recap

Here's an at-a-glance summary of the strategies we've discussed to help kids at various ages independently access their capacity to sleep.

- **Birth to Six Weeks.** Know that your baby will sleep most of the time, waking every few hours to be fed. Do your best to create a quiet environment for sleep.

- **Six Weeks Onward.** Establish a soothing bedtime ritual. Begin to establish routines for naps and at night.

- **Four to Six Months.** If your baby isn't sleeping through the night, try the Weissbluth or adapted Ferber method every single night for a week. If teething disrupts the child's sleep, try again once the tooth erupts.

- **Seven to Twelve Months.** Add a verbal component to your bedtime ritual, such as saying good night to special toys or to the sun and moon. If schedule changes disturb sleep patterns, repeat the sleep training method. If you used the Ferber process, try Weissbluth's less time-consuming extinction method. Expect to repeat sleep training a number of times as your child grows.

- **Eighteen to Twenty-Four Months.** If your child climbs out of the crib, it's time to graduate to a big kid's bed. Let her sleep on the crib mattress on the floor until you can buy an appropriate bed.

- **Twelve to Thirty-Six Months.** Toddlers may resist being left alone to sleep. Anticipate needs (fear of dark, thirst, bathroom) and build them into a consistent bedtime ritual. Let a child (over twelve months) choose a few toys to sleep with.

If necessary, sit in the child's darkened room until she dozes off, but each night move closer to the door until you're out of the room. Avoid conversation. Repeat the mantra: "I love you. I know you can do this. Now it's time to relax and go to sleep."

- **Two to Six Years.** Child-proof your house with gates on stairs (if needed) and locks on windows. Resist welcoming your child into your bed; turn her around and walk—don't carry—her back to bed. Keep saying, "You're a big kid now, and big kids sleep in their own beds."

CHAPTER 2

The Comfort Zone: Self-Soothing Without Props

Meeting a friend for lunch, I arrived a little early and was seated next to two young women. I was checking my email, tuning out their conversation, but with the tables so close I couldn't help but overhear. Sharing photos, they were comparing notes on their kids. "Joey's got a new trick," I heard one say. "It's driving us a little crazy."

The other mom laughed.

"For weeks he was sleeping really well," her friend went on. "We'd pop in his binky and he'd fall right to sleep. If he woke up crying, we'd just plug it back in—no problem. But now he's almost six months old, so he's realized that spitting out his pacifier will get our attention."

We started putting a few extras in his crib, even showing him where they were. No luck!

"Now, when he starts crying, we go in, and there are all the binkies on the floor. I think he gets a kick out of lobbing them just so we come running."

"That's so classic," her friend said. "Such a smart kid! What can you do?"

To Plug or Not to Plug

Many parents struggle with the decision of whether or not to offer their child a pacifier. Not every baby will accept one, but for those who do, it sure can come in handy. Most importantly, research shows that pacifier use may reduce SIDS risks. That's why the American Academy of Pediatrics encourages parents to offer (but never force acceptance of) pacifiers at naptime and bedtime to babies under a year old.[1] As a pediatrician and the mother of two children, I am not opposed to them at all. However, I do advise parents to delay the introduction of pacifiers until after breast feeding is well established so as to not interfere with proper "latching" of the baby's mouth to the nipple and, ultimately, long-term breast-feeding success.

If used properly, pacifiers can also offer certain benefits. Of course, distracting or calming a cranky baby by engaging his powerful sucking reflex is a major one. Many parents feel that, since a pacifier is removable, it can promote less of a dependency than fingers and thumbs. Its use is more easily restricted to certain situations, like sleeping, and it is also easier for parents to take it away when the time comes.

For babies from birth to nine months old, I see the pacifier as a welcome source of comfort when a parent isn't holding or rocking them. It's something they can reach for at four or five months old, when they feel that they would like some soothing. It helps bridge the gap while they're learning other self-comforting techniques as they grow.

Think about it: managing stress is an essential skill for adults. We've all developed a repertoire of coping mechanisms, like phoning a friend to blow off steam, taking a brisk walk, listening to music, meditating, and practicing deep breathing or yoga, to name just a few. Over the course of a lifetime, your child will have to develop his own palette of age-appropriate calming strategies.

For a new baby, there aren't many options for comfort beyond eating and cuddling. When your child reaches out for a pacifier, he's problem solving, coming up with a strategy to satisfy his need to suck and soothe. As he learns that it makes him feel calm, he will look for it when he needs it. This is a step toward independence, as it's a means for a child to calm himself without needing the assistance of an adult.

Don't be surprised if your baby initially resists a pacifier. I recommend first introducing it when your child isn't hungry, to spare him the frustration of sucking without getting any milk. It can take a little practice for a child to learn to use a pacifier. At first, many children have difficulty keeping one in their mouths. It's okay if you have to hold it in place until he gets the hang of it. You may have to try different varieties until you find the one that suits your baby best.

If your baby's pacifier falls out and he doesn't fuss, don't feel that you need to replace it. He will let you know when he needs it, and as he gets older, you can encourage him to reach for it himself.

If after a few tries, your baby really doesn't want a pacifier, don't push it. You may find that he discovers his thumb or comes up with other ways to soothe himself. Either way, he has voiced his opinion and taken a step toward independence!

There are a few downsides of using a pacifier that deserve mention. First, the habit of using one eventually has to be broken. While I generally discourage starting routines that will have to be halted later on, the short-term benefits of pacifier use often outweigh this disadvantage. Quitting the pacifier is usually not that hard for children under a year old. Kids are resilient, and by that time, most have learned new ways to entertain themselves and calm down when overstimulated.

Pacifiers get dirty when dropped. When that happens, resist popping the pacifier into your mouth to "clean" it before returning it to your child. Your mouth contains bacteria that, among other things, can give your child cavities. Warm, soapy water or carrying extra pacifiers with you are better alternatives.

The other thing to consider about pacifier use is making sure that it doesn't get in the way of development. As early as three months old, your baby will start experimenting with making sounds and the way they feel in his mouth by cooing and actively vocalizing. That's not easy to do if his mouth is constantly plugged, so try to only make the pacifier available during times when it's really needed.

By six to nine months, the benefits of pacifier use are less pronounced, while at the same time your baby's babbling will start sounding more like "real" language, as he begins forming syllables and imitating your speech rhythms. You can encourage and facilitate these exciting efforts by minimizing pacifier use—ideally limiting it to only during sleep—while at the same time spending more of his waking hours reading to him, singing with him, and talking to him. He is sure to absorb and revel in your words and intonations.

Regardless of how pacifier dependent or disinterested your baby is during his first year, by the time your child steps into toddlerhood and is ready to really start babbling and then talking, the pacifier, beneficial in earlier months, becomes much more of an impediment to his independence. This is especially true when it's offered/used during waking hours and thus interferes with self-expression. That's why I recommend limiting it to the crib.

As my lunch-table neighbors observed, it can also become a bid for parental attention. If you become the nighttime pacifier

The Binky Bylaws

Nature has given babies a powerful sucking drive, which many engage for self-soothing between feedings. If your baby finds it comforting, let her use a pacifier, but keep these guidelines in mind.

- **Do be aware that offering babies a pacifier to suck on as they fall asleep is thought to be protective against SIDS.**

- **Do offer her the pacifier at naptime and bedtime, as well as at times of stress.** By limiting pacifier use to definite times, you'll teach her that there are distinct periods in the day for playing, learning, and socialization, as well as lulls when it's appropriate to cool down with a comforting pacifier.

- **Do make sure that you and other caretakers are on the same page when it comes to pacifier use.** If your mother-in-law or a nanny is overly pacifier permissive, your limiting and weaning efforts will be that much harder to accomplish.

police, you give your child a foolproof way to repeatedly lure you to his bedside. If your child's pacifier should fall out during the night, let him come up with a solution—whether to reach out and put it back in or figure out how to fall asleep without it. Certainly, a child like Joey, with the coordination to yank out his pacifier and fling it, was capable of deciding to replace it with one of the others in his crib! However, in order to make that decision, he had to learn that the pacifier police weren't always going to rush to his rescue.

The Binky Bylaws sidebar below offers some of the dos and don'ts of pacifier use.

- **Do set a definite date to wean your child off the pacifier—** ideally, before her first birthday. It's much harder to wrestle a beloved pacifier from an older child.

- **Don't use the pacifier as a babysitter—**that is, don't let your child stay plugged up all day long for the sake of peace. During waking hours, your baby has essential work to do: practicing language, interacting with you and others, learning to play, discovering what she likes, exploring, crawling, scooting, and so on. It's her job to begin to negotiate life, just as it's your job to engage and stimulate her.

- **Don't pop the pacifier into your child's mouth for your own convenience,** like when a friend calls or when you're making dinner. Strive for consistency, tempered by compassionate assessment of your child's true needs.

- **Don't put the pacifier on a cord** around your child's neck or attach it to her clothing or crib rails with string, which can pose a strangling hazard.

Unplugging

When should you—and how do you—wean your child from his pacifier? There are some who believe that two years old is the definite cutoff point. However, in my experience as a pediatrician—not to mention with my own children—it is far better to make the transition sooner, around nine to twelve months of age. While there's no hard and fast rule, I can tell you from lots of experience that it does not get any easier as kids get older!

In large part, this is because a younger child will be less fiercely resistant to surrendering the pacifier. When a child becomes old enough to start making his own declarations of independence and to demand a pacifier, it will be harder to change his mind. It can be a real challenge to come out on top of a power struggle with a toddler.

But, of course, the bigger reason to pull the pacifier sooner rather than later is to empower your child to find other ways to comfort and soothe himself. At nine months, he has the developmental skills to do so. This is a major achievement! Not to mention the importance of developing his vocabulary and using it to interact. This is an exciting period of sound formation—an important step toward speech development.

For a child under a year old, I have found that the most effective way to withdraw a pacifier is simply to "pull the plug." Ideally, he'll be using it mostly at naptime and bedtime (see the Binky Bylaws, page 52). If it's his constant companion, you may need to spend a week or two limiting its use to pre-sleep periods. This may not be easy for him, but fortunately babies at this age can be distracted easily. You may need to be a more active presence in his playtime during these weeks until he figures out how to entertain himself without the aid of his pacifier.

Then, choose a night, preferably on a three-day weekend or over a short vacation, to begin weaning. Be sure that your partner (and/or any of your child's caregivers) is amenable, because you may have to tough out a few nights of indignant resistance to your plan. I firmly believe that cold-turkey pacifier withdrawal is both more effective and, ultimately, kinder than sporadically giving in. If you succumb, you'll be teaching your child that he'll get the pacifier if he just cries long and hard enough. That unintended and undesirable message will spell misery for you, for him, and for everyone else in the house.

Instead, simply keep in mind that you're not cruelly depriving him but freeing him from a habit that has the distinct ability to become firmly ingrained and inhibit social development. Rest assured that liberation can take as little as two or three days.

> "I guess that chucking pacifiers means that it's weaning time," said Joey's mother. "Someone told me to cut the tip off the binky, so he won't like sucking it as much."
>
> I opened my mouth to interrupt and protest, but luckily, her friend intervened. "Don't even think of trying that," she insisted—emphatically, and correctly. "I heard that too when I was weaning Sheila, but my pediatrician said, 'No way.' Pieces can come off. It's a real choking risk."
>
> "I hadn't thought of that—thanks for telling me," Joey's mother replied. "What did you do with Sheila?"
>
> "I just stopped giving her the pacifier, and she got over it," her friend said very matter-of-factly. "It actually wasn't as hard as I thought it was going to be. We had two bad nights and that was it."

Toddler Detachment

If you are the parent of a toddler who's already firmly attached to her pacifier, you can expect more resistance at weaning time than a younger child can muster, but all is not lost. You will simply need to take a bit of a different approach to prepare her for "Good-bye, Pacie" day.

If she's a constant pacifier user, you might want to have her begin to cut down a few weeks in advance. You can start by limiting the times and places she can have it—only at naptime and bedtime, only in her room. Be kind about it. While she may be more attached and therefore more resistant, the advantage of weaning an older child is that she can listen to at least a certain degree of reason. Explain that she's a big girl now and that it's exciting to let go of baby gear.

Guide her to find alternative comforting objects, like a favorite stuffed toy or book, which she can keep with her when she's out of her room, enjoying the rest of the family. If she really wants the pacifier, tell her that she's free to go off and use it in her room. This often works quite well, as toddlers typically like nothing more than to be a part of the "party" and the last thing they want is to be excluded from what's going on. That said, let it be her decision, and don't criticize her choice. When she's done with the pacifier and comes out of her room, be sure to welcome her warmly.

At bedtime, you can ask her, "What will help you go to sleep? Your teddy bear? Your nightlight? Some music? Some books?" Give her a few choices to start her thinking, but ultimately let her come up with the solution. By doing so, you'll instill the concept that it is her responsibility to get herself to sleep—and give her a vote of confidence, showing that you know she can do it. Remember that sleep is not something that you can impose; it's a capacity that she has to find within herself. By having her choose the method (within reason, of course), you'll be reinforcing the fact there are myriad ways to soothe oneself—a lesson that will be of use to her through life.

Along the way, explain what you'll do with the pacifiers. Some parents find success by telling their children they get to box them up and mail them off to all the babies of the world! Whatever you decide, be sure to engage your child in the plan—get her excited about it—then make a ceremony on the big day. Invite the family over. Let her do something creative, like decorate the box (you can wrap it and have her draw pictures on it, and family members can add their own drawings). Then, when the party winds down, get the box out of the house. Have someone take it home to "mail" it, or even bring your child to the post office to send it off to the babies (aka, to grandma's or a friend's house). At bedtime, you don't want that box in the house, for there may be pleas or tears that will shake your resolve and make you tear it open.

It may take a few days, but rest assured, your child will quickly rebound from missing her pacifier—especially if you've helped her learn how to find other ways to fall asleep independently. Be strong and be patient. Keep reminding her that she's embarking on the great adventure of growing up. Remind her of all the "big girl" activities and privileges that will be open to her now that she's not a baby anymore.

Safety Note: Some people suggest cutting off the tip of the pacifier (as in the anecdote on page 55) as a way to make the pacifier less desirable to the child. I want to reiterate that this is not a good idea and can be dangerous. Young children can choke on pieces of the pacifier, so I strongly caution against this technique.

Sibling Setbacks

A new sibling can create an unanticipated challenge when it comes to staying off of the pacifier. A child who has been fine without one for months can often decide she wants it back. This is precisely what the woman sitting in the coffee shop described below feared.

> "What I'm worried about now," the friend was saying, "is how Sheila will react if I give her baby sister a pacifier. Clara is two months old now, so I have to decide what to do pretty soon."
>
> "Oh no," said Joey's mother.
>
> "She's pretty good with Clara. She pats and kisses her, but she does seem jealous of all the attention Clara gets. I have to be sure to give Sheila extra cuddling and praise for things, like putting her teddy bear to bed. She's coping, but I wonder if seeing Clara get a pacifier will be too much for her."
>
> "Maybe she just won't want one," Joey's mother said hopefully.
>
> "Fingers crossed," he friend replied. "I'm holding off on giving Clara a pacifier, at least for now."

It can indeed be rough for an older child if a new baby gets a pacifier. Let's face it: The new sibling is already basking in affection, being constantly cuddled and fed. It can be like adding insult to injury if the baby is also allowed to enjoy a binky.

I see this dynamic frequently in my office. When there is a new a baby in the house, many older siblings want to return to babyhood themselves. What better way is there to act like a baby than to use a pacifier?

I wouldn't have told Sheila's mother that she had to hold off on giving Clara a pacifier for Sheila's sake, especially in light of what we know about pacifiers' potential protective effects against SIDS when used as babies are falling asleep during the early months. But she was right to anticipate wailing. If your child is old enough to speak, you'll almost certainly hear howls. The child will be right, of course. It isn't fair, but sometimes life isn't. The reality of being an older sibling in a family is that the baby will be held more, be fed rather than feed herself, be carried or pushed in a stroller, and so on. As a parent, all you can do is stay compassionate and keep highlighting how special it is to be older.

You can say, "You know, pacifiers are for babies. You're past that now and on to big-boy things. Let's do something that the baby isn't old enough to do. What should that be?"

Maybe the answer is a special trip to the park, a book you can read together, or some little toy you can share, like a puzzle you can watch (or help) him assemble to give him an extra dose of attention. By making it his decision, you're showing him that he has a full palette of ways to comfort himself, without relying on just one prop. (Of course, you'll still want to be on the lookout for the occasional binky snatch.) You're underscoring that independent action is a greater privilege than a pacifier.

Finger Suckers

Many children who never took to pacifiers suck their fingers or their thumbs. These habits can be challenging for parents because they can't take away fingers and thumbs. There's no way to put them in a box and ship them off to other babies!

It's nearly impossible to limit the amount of time an infant spends with her thumb in her mouth. During awake times, you can certainly offer her rattles and toys to distract her, but when she gets sleepy, you may find that her thumb inevitably creeps into her mouth. And this is okay.

Your mother and your friends may have opinions about thumb sucking, but I don't think it's all that productive to start limiting it until the child is four years old. At that age, you can reason with her and give her a meaningful choice, as you would when limiting her pacifier use.

You can say, "Michelle, I see that you want to suck your thumb right now. That's all right. But thumb sucking is something that we do in private. So go ahead, if you want, and suck your thumb in your room. When you are ready, wipe off your thumb then come out and play with me."

Why is this approach so effective? For one thing, it sidesteps a potential power struggle and the scolding and nagging that may have the paradoxical effect of encouraging her to seek comfort by sucking. For another, it doesn't rely on the external motivations that some advocate, like painting her fingers or thumb with foul-tasting nail polish or offering her bribes to stop sucking them. These strategies might work, but they don't promote the child's growth. Giving Michelle the power to decide what to do teaches her a lesson transcending the immediate issue of thumb and finger sucking: it shows her that actions have consequences and that it's up to her to choose which consequences she can accept.

You're letting her weigh for herself the comfort of thumb sucking versus the pleasure of social interaction. You're showing her concretely that playing and being with the family are activities that deserve her full attention. Without the distraction of a mouthful of thumb or fingers, she'll be more able to focus on engaging with others (and actually using her hands), which is, of course, a critical developmental step.

There will be times when Michelle will want to go to her room and suck her thumb. Then, given the choice, she will soon want to come back to the much more fulfilling option: connecting with the rest of the family. There's no contest!

What about substitute comfort objects, like the blankets that some kids adopt after surrendering (or instead of) pacifiers? They don't plug the mouth and therefore don't hinder speech. Even so, in toddlerhood, you'll also want to start limiting their use to the bedroom or to certain times of day. A child who's always dragging a blanket around isn't focused on exploring new skills through play. When she starts preschool, that comfort object will likely interfere with her activities. Do you really want your child trying to finger paint while clutching her blankie?

Of course you don't. I can certainly understand parents' reluctance to separate their kids from precious objects, especially ones that don't do obvious harm. But your goal is to guide your child toward discovering her own competencies. When the props of childhood start to get in the way, it's time to leave them behind. Children grow and change quickly; it won't take long before Bunny and Blankie are supplanted by tea sets and miniature race cars.

Letting go is not so much a loss as an adventure, a step into self-determination and ultimately a chance for your child to discover what gives her pleasure and comfort independently.

The Comfort Zone Recap

Here's an at-a-glance review of ways to encourage children to comfort themselves at various ages:

- **Birth to Four Months.** Once breast feeding is well-established, offer a pacifier at naptime and bedtime or when baby needs soothing. It's okay to hold it until he learns to suck it. Never force a pacifier on him.

- **Four to Nine Months.** Limit pacifier use to crib time and, perhaps, in the car seat on long trips. Don't use the pacifier for your convenience. Stimulate language development by talking and responding to your baby. When your child plays games with the pacifier, don't retrieve and return it to him.

- **Nine Months to Twelve Months.** Limit pacifier use to naptime and bedtime. Let him choose an alternative comfort object when not in the crib. (He should not *sleep* with this object until he's twelve months old). After a week or two, put him to bed without the pacifier. His wailing, mercifully, should subside within two or three days.

- **Over Twelve Months.** Weaning may be more difficult. Limit pacifier use to bedtime and naptime for a few weeks. If he insists on using a pacifier at other times, allow him to do it privately, in the bedroom. Emphasize the excitement of growing up, which means leaving the pacifier behind. Choose a date for weaning and celebrate it with a special treat.

- **Over Two Years.** Make it a real family celebration. Pack the pacifiers in a box to mail to the babies of the world!

CHAPTER 3

The Food Fight: Mealtime

Lois brought in two-year-old Jared for his well-child checkup. Jared was all smiles, bouncy, and fun. He was big for his age and seemed healthy. But Lois said that she was concerned about Jared's diet.

"I can't get him to eat much," she told me. "All he seems to want is milk and juice, plus goldfish crackers and dry Cheerios. Of course, I know that he needs vegetables and protein, but he won't eat any real food anymore. He hates to sit still for meals these days and just wants to snack on the run. . . . I'm so worried about his diet, and every meal becomes a battle!"

Jared was acting like a typical toddler. When children become responsible for the food that goes in their mouths, their eating habits often change. And with Jared's newfound motor skills, he was always on the go. Couple that with the development of food preferences and the ability to say, "No," and you have a picky toddler who no longer eats nutritious meals. The food fight was on!

Toddlerhood is prime time for power struggles of all kinds, so it's no surprise when meals become a battleground. It's frustrating, and it's especially worrisome for parents when a kid who's had a normal interest in food grows fussy and starts resisting meals. Thinking longer term, the parents picture a grim future of pasta, pizza, and the occasional round of chicken nuggets instead of the healthy fare that they'd prefer to feed their child.

Luckily, for many toddlers, food resistance is a phase and not the first step in an inevitable march to the steady diet of starchy, fatty, sweet, or salty white foods with minimal nutrients. And, as I told Lois, by curtailing Jared's constant grazing (as well as his sugary-juice habit), she could not only reengage his interest in meals but also guide him toward more nourishing food choices. Note that I said "guide him," not "impose food on him." The most effective way to promote a healthy diet to a child is to make it his responsibility—to give him a range of options that he can choose independently and come to enjoy. Later in this chapter, we'll discuss these options, for the kinds of food and the way they're offered to heighten their child appeal.

Eating is such a basic life function that it is a major area in which a child will try—and be able—to establish mastery, starting in early infancy.

Bottle Basics

Most babies, when being cuddled and fed, will touch the mother's breast or play with her hair. When bottle feeding, many will reach for the bottle and curl their fingers around it. It's part of a natural impulse to explore the world with their hands. They may not actually know what they're doing, but the urge to discover is there, very early on.

Many babies as young as three months old will have the motor skills to actually grasp a bottle and soon will to try to hold it on their own. If your child is not grabbing at her bottle by five or six months old, you should encourage her placing her hands around it. Of course, it may take a little practice before a child can not only clutch but also stabilize an object. You'll have to help her hold it and then remove your fingers briefly now and then until she gets the hang of it.

Learning to hold a bottle is a major developmental step. Yes, having her hold the bottle will allow you to put her down a little more often, but that's not the reason to do it. It's the first move toward having a child who can feed herself.

Safety Note 1: Even if your baby is fully at ease with the bottle, able to tip it up, and remove it from her mouth at will, *always* supervise her feedings. You should never just walk away but rather take delight in her accomplishment. You can also continue to cradle her in your arms while she supports the bottle in her hands.

Safety Note 2: Never prop a bottle in a baby's crib, car seat, or bouncy seat. It's too easy for the baby to choke on the contents. Your eyes should be on her at all times when she's eating or drinking. Remember, the goal is not to free your hands (that's just an added bonus) but to show your child that she has the skills to hold the bottle on her own.

A baby who can hold a bottle still needs you. She needs the quiet time you spend cuddled together during feedings, when you gaze into her eyes, talking sweetly. Those bonding moments remain critical to her development, even as she's mastering new skills. I loved snuggling my babies while they ate, and once they held their own bottles, loved having a free hand to stroke them. But it also thrilled me to see them coming into their own, embracing their own powers through the sophisticated movements of grabbing, clutching, and balancing a bottle.

By around nine months old, most babies will able to maneuver the bottle on their own, especially if you've been helping them practice, supporting the bottle while they grasp it and letting go now and then to let them hold it on their own. Gradually, they will come to understand what you're teaching them to do. That being said, it's not really cause for alarm if the bottle-holding concept seems to elude your baby. The experience of Anna, the mother of my eight-month-old patient Carly, is not uncommon.

> "I keep trying to teach her," Anna said. "But she doesn't seem to want to tip the bottle upright. Maybe it's too heavy for her? I'm worried that when I let her hold it herself, all she gets is a mouthful of air."
>
> "Hmmm," I said. "I doubt that the bottle is too heavy."
>
> "Do you think she just wants me to feed her?" Anna asked. "She doesn't even try to lift the bottle enough to keep it filled with milk."

"I've seen other children just like Carly," I told her. "For whatever reason, they don't like leaning back to make it easy to tip up the bottle. The position she's in when you cradle her to feed her feels comfortable and familiar. But since she's already eight months old, I'd let the bottle training go. She'd be better off learning to use a sippy cup at her age."

A week later Anna called to report that Carly was fascinated with her sippy cup. "She likes holding it and seems a bit surprised when I demonstrate that milk comes out of the straw part. But I think she's beginning to understand."

I encourage parents, whether they breast- or bottle-feed, to introduce babies to different kinds of sippy cups around the age of six months old. While that's too soon for most to master them, even playing with empty ones awakens kids to the potential of the big, wide world beyond the breast or bottle. I typically recommend the kind with the straw attached because a baby can try sucking it in comfortable positions. She doesn't have to tilt backward as she would to hold and drink from a bottle.

A major benefit of this kind of sippy cup is that sucking a straw strengthens the child's cheek muscles. Many speech therapists like these cups, as opposed to some other types of sippy cups and bottles. Bonus point: most restaurants have straws with "to-go" cup covers. If your child can drink from a straw, you will have one less item to pack in the diaper bag!

I like to see babies completely weaned from bottle feeding by the time they're twelve to fifteen months old. There are lots of good reasons to make this shift as soon as possible. A big one is that you want your toddler to be motivated to eat solid food. In my experience, bottle-fed babies tend to drink more milk, which sometimes reduces their intake of solids. Another is that it is usually much easier to refocus a younger child than a head-strong toddler who keeps demanding, "Ba-ba, ba-ba, ba-ba."

Making the Bottle-to-Cup Transition

For most parents, the transition to a cup goes easier than they anticipated. They fear the dreaded day, procrastinate for many months, and then are pleasantly surprised at how easily it goes. However, there are some children who are really fond of their bottles and outright refuse to drink milk from a cup, sometimes hurling the milk-filled cup across the room.

Here are the strategies I suggest for making the bottle-to-cup transition:

- **Avoid Overattachment to Bottle.** Don't let your child get overly attached to his bottle—lugging it with him all the time, taking it to bed. Constant use makes it harder to break his dependence. Reserve these for mealtimes.

- **Begin Transition from Bottle to Cup Early.** Begin the transition from bottle to cup once your child enjoys solid food. In the beginning, he will likely just play with the cup and toss it on the ground, but one day its purpose will click and he'll use it with ease. The earlier you start him on the sippy cup, the easier the transition will be.

- **Put Milk or Formula in Cup.** Put whatever the child is used to drinking from the bottle—breast milk or formula—into the sippy cup. It's comforting for a child to discover that the contents of the new container are familiar. Besides, if you use the sippy cup for water and keep the bottle for milk, he will associate just the bottle with milk and will always want to drink from it.

- **Begin with the Cup.** Once your child accepts the cup, begin each feeding session with it, substituting the breast or bottle only when he gets frustrated.

- **Find the Right Cup.** Experiment with different cups until you find one that your child likes. The model with the attached straw is my favorite, but even these come in different styles, like with or without handles.

- **Eliminate Nighttime Bottle.** Expect the nighttime bottle to be the hardest to eliminate—maybe more for you than for your child. So many parents tell me how much they dread dropping that bottle and then are shocked at how quickly their kids rebound. After a couple of days, most don't even miss it. It can help to start extricating the bottle from the bedtime ritual by offering it earlier in the evening, followed by tooth brushing.

You'll note that in the discussion above, I've mentioned only breast milk, formula, and water, though some parents will put juice in the sippy cup. Many kids do love sweet beverages, but I don't recommend offering infants juice. It only gets them used to sugary drinks that are full of nonnutritional calories.

I don't think my own kids ever tasted juice until they were offered juice boxes at a birthday party. By then, they were old enough to view juice, like other sweets, as something to consume in moderation. I tell parents to limit their kids' consumption to four ounces of 100 percent juice per day. If they are tempted to give them more, they should dilute the juice with water. I prefer that children eat whole fruit and find that most really enjoy it.

Solid Food

When is your baby ready for solid food? According to American Academy of Pediatrics' guidelines, the time comes between four and six months of age, once your child has established good head control and seems interested in what you eat.[1] She may even signal her readiness by grabbing at your food. At your baby's four-month checkup, ask your pediatrician if it's time to make the leap.

Your child may need some practice before she can swallow solids. Remember that before now, your baby had a reflex to prevent choking: if there was something textured in her mouth, her tongue would stick out. Now she has to learn that sensing texture on her tongue means that her tongue should move backward so she can swallow. Her grimaces may suggest that she doesn't like the food, but rest assured, these are just signs that she's developing her swallowing skill.

Expect the learning process to be gradual, and if your baby doesn't get the hang of swallowing food initially, don't push her. Stay calm but persistent. You don't want your baby to sense stress around mealtimes. This should be an exciting milestone!

Start your baby on a single-grain baby cereal, just after a serving of formula or breast milk. There isn't really any scientific evidence that shows that cereal should be the first food, but traditionally this is what most parents choose. To begin, I don't recommend a set amount of cereal or a specific ratio of cereal to milk. Every baby is different and can handle varying amounts and textures. A good rule of thumb is to mix a few tablespoons of cereal with enough formula or breast milk to reach a yogurt-like consistency. If she gobbles it up, give some more the next time. If you overshoot, give her less until she seems eager for more.

When your baby starts on solids, offer her breast milk or formula beforehand, as it will be her major source of nutrition. After her milk course, give her as much cereal as she likes. Babies are amazing self-regulators and will turn their heads away when they are finished. Start with one meal of cereal per day, and increase to two and then three as your child gets more acclimated. Once your child has mastered the sippy cup, you can start the shift to offering milk alongside the meal rather than beforehand. After all, that's how adults eat.

Note: Many parents have heard that putting cereal in a baby's last nighttime bottle will help her sleep longer. In my experience, this is a myth. Cereal at night will not affect your child's sleep. Don't give the baby diluted cereal in a bottle unless specifically directed by your doctor. The goal is to teach her to eat solid food, not to sneak in cereal in liquid form.

Besides cereal, what and how much solid food should your child eat? When should foods be introduced and in what order? These questions and myriad others vex parents from birth onward. When expanding your child's diet, the place to start is with your pediatrician.

I tell my patients that there are no strict rules about how to begin the process. There are books describing which foods to introduce first, the exact amounts to offer, in what order, and at what time of day. After talking to your doctor, come up with a plan that makes sense to you and seems to be right for your child. The most important thing is that both you and your child enjoy the feeding process.

A Few Guidelines for Introducing Solid Foods

Here are a few of my guidelines: Between four and six months you can start solid foods (although they are really soft, mushy foods). As mentioned earlier, most parents start with a single-grain cereal, although there really aren't hard and fast rules for what that first food should be. By the time your child is five to six months old, you can broaden her palate by introducing fruits and vegetables. I personally don't think it matters which comes first and what order you choose. I often suggest introducing a few easily portable foods, like bananas and avocados, so you don't always have to lug around heavy baby food jars. Besides, many restaurants have these items on hand, so you may not even have to bring them along. Then ask for a to-go cup with a straw and there are two less items for the diaper bag! The First-Year Food Fest sidebar on page 74 offers some helpful tips for introducing your baby to solids.

Anytime from about six months to eight months old, your baby will take an interest in the feeding process, grabbing at the spoon or paddling in the food bowl then, missing her mouth, smearing food all over her face. Some will even refuse to be fed, insisting on "feeding" themselves. Don't discourage these explorations, messy as they are. Your baby is showing initiative. Praise her efforts!

Try giving her a little spoon of her own, filled with things like mashed potatoes, mashed bananas, thick cereal, or baby food—gooey enough to stick to the spoon but not gluey enough to make her gag—for her to use while you slip alternate helpings of food into her mouth. Once she is eight to ten months old, you might also give some her easy-to-grasp foods (like thin strips of toast) that she can clutch and gum or use to test out her newly erupting teeth. With a collaborative approach, until she gets the hang of it, you'll get enough food into her (supplemented by breast milk or formula) while acknowledging and satisfying her healthy need for independence.

Initially, most babies are "palmers" and "rakers" as they try to feed themselves. Simply put, this means that they clutch

The First-Year Food Fest

Most parents take delight in starting solid foods and come to my office eager and excited to get started. Here are a few guidelines for those first foods.

- **Avoid Choking Hazards and Honey.** When your baby is beyond six months old, you can introduce him to almost any food you like, with two important exceptions—choking hazards and honey. Do not give your baby honey until he is a year old. Honey may expose your baby to botulism, a serious illness. Children over one year of age are better able to resist the risks of botulism.

- **Watch for Dangerous Shapes and Textures.** Watch out for shapes and consistencies that can cause choking, such as popcorn, gluey foods like peanut butter, hard vegetables like carrots, and whole grapes.

- **Hold Off on Whole Milk.** Wait to give your child cow's milk until his first birthday, though you can give him yogurt and cheese food in the palms of their hands or shovel it into their mouths but have not yet mastered the more useful and precise skill of picking up items using a thumb and forefinger. Referred to as a *pincer grasp*, this fine motor milestone typically develops around nine months. So scatter a few finger foods, like a handful of cooked peas, finely chopped bananas, baby friendly cereal, or puffs on her high-chair tray to encourage pincer practice.

And it does take practice: think of the complex of skills involved in aiming for a pea, grabbing or otherwise trying to propel it into your hand (ideally, working your thumb and finger together to secure it), raising it to your face without dropping

from six months onward. Continue to give him breast milk or formula during his first year.

- **Note Food Allergies.** We used to tell parents to delay foods that were more likely to cause allergies, like eggs, strawberries, and peanut products, until the first year or even beyond, but at the time of this writing, this is no longer the recommendation unless there is a strong family history of food allergies or if your child is prone to eczema.

- **Experiment with Finger Foods.** At eight to ten months, your child can experiment with small finger foods. If she seems to gag on them, wait a little longer. Start with a food like a puff that easily dissolves, to avoid choking.

- **Buy or Make Food.** You can either buy or make your child's food. There's nothing magical about store-bought baby food, so if you want to puree a little homemade chicken along with your child's vegetable, go right ahead! Just be sure that the consistency is smooth and thin enough for easy swallowing.

it, and inserting it directly into the vicinity of your mouth and releasing it. Whew! But we've all learned to do it, and your baby will too. As you see her struggle (sticking her whole fist into her mouth to deliver the pea), resist the temptation to just pop it in yourself to save time. She deserves to take all the time she needs to master this important milestone.

Of course, what I've just described is an ideal scenario. Many babies are eager to feed themselves but can't quite sync their abilities and desires. They get cranky and frustrated when they can't quite grip food or maneuver it into their mouths. All you should do is lay on the praise and lovingly encourage them to keep trying. This phase will pass fairly quickly. Most self-starter babies will be feeding themselves with gusto by ten to sixteen months old.

There are also plenty of babies who'd rather not lift a finger. They prefer to sit back and be fed, even when they have the motor skills to do it themselves. If given finger foods, they play with them or fling them to the floor. They bang on their high chairs, flipping food off their spoons rather than trying to move the spoons to their mouths. Such babies may have more laid-back personalities or just lack the impetus at the moment to try something new. If your baby reaches twelve months old and shows little interest in self-feeding, be patient. Chances are, all she needs is a firm but gentle push to embrace her skills. I say "gentle" because stressing over children's developmental stages is not productive. It can keep kids, who sense your anxiety, entrenched in the familiar routines that you hope they'll change.

A Few Recommendations on Self-Feeding

If your child seems to have mealtime inertia, a quick glance at any parenting blog will show that you're not alone. Naturally, those blogs are full of suggestions for encouraging self-feeding, but here are the recommendations that I offer to parents for children eight to ten months old who are well-coordinated graspers and can swallow solids easily:

- **Model Eating.** Model the pleasures and motions of eating for your child. Have her watch you eat a spoonful of food, a palmful of dry cereal, and some pinches of berries while smiling and making sounds of enjoyment, like, "Mmm, mmm." Talk her through the eating process. Do it often.

- **Save the Cup Until Last.** When introducing or encouraging your child to eat table foods, don't be too quick to offer her tried-and-true sippy cup to her if she feigns interest in her food—save that for last. Instead, put some clutchable foods, like toast strips, on her high-chair tray. You can show her what to do by putting a strip in her hand, then raising her hand to her mouth so that she can take a bite. If she doesn't get the message, do it yourself to demonstrate. Then back off, staying nearby but not rushing to feed her. Give her a chance to experiment.

- **Help Your Child Learn to Eat.** Load up her spoon, put it in her hand, and then raise spoon and hand to her mouth, letting her take a mouthful of food. Reload the spoon, and then step back to give her a chance to mimic the action.

- **Demonstrate How to Pick Up Food.** Demonstrate how she can push her thumb and finger together to capture a small object, like a pea. If she waits for you to pop it in her mouth, don't do it. Taking yourself out of the feeding equation will deliver the message that she can learn to eat without you.

- **Know That Self-Feeding Takes Time.** Like most developmental milestones, self-feeding won't become a fully ingrained habit the instant your child learns to do it. There may be backslides—times when she's tired or, for some other reason, just wants to be fed. But try not to succumb very often, especially with an older child who's been resistant. Keep praising and encouraging her until it becomes second nature for her to feed herself.

That said, anytime you have a concern about your child's development, be sure to check in with your child's pediatrician.

The Toddler Nosh

When your child is around one year old, you may notice a change in his appetite.

As Lois observed with Jared, the exploring and experimenting of the years from one to three can distract toddlers from eating. Furthermore, newly-minted one-year-olds are feeling their own powers, and choosing how to eat is a way for them to take control. The challenge for parents is therefore to resist making meals a power struggle, or else succumbing, as Lois and so many other parents do, by letting them play while filling up on milk and snack foods.

One major line of defense against toddler distraction is the family meal. As toddlers and kindergartners grow increasingly able to eat the grown-up food, ideally they're also going to be developing the social skills necessary to interact with and enjoy the family. Having a toddler running around and grazing all the time not only limits him to finger foods but also deprives him of the chance to participate in family life.

Of course, many of us can't put a full, sit-down family meal on the table every night, but it's well worth making the effort to do so when we can. Young toddlers usually need dinner sooner than six or seven o'clock, when adults are ready to eat. You'll want to feed your toddler something earlier, when he's naturally hungry, but then it's a good idea whenever possible to serve him dinner while the adults are eating. This will underscore the notion that there's a place to eat (at the table) and a way to eat (sitting down), instilling the idea that eating is not a haphazard activity to accomplish on the run but a meaningful ritual.

Of course, you can't expect your toddler to sit still for the entire duration of a relaxed (that is, longer-lasting) meal. Some will, but most, especially those under the age of two, are doing well if they manage to last more than five or ten minutes. That's okay. Don't force your child to sit there, but also don't let getting up and down from the table become a game.

That's what Lois did with Jared. To increase the likelihood that Jared would be hungry and amenable to the idea of sitting down for dinner, she started by limiting his juice intake to about four ounces a day. Then she put him on a daily schedule of three meals and two snacks, which he could eat only when he was sitting down rather than have him graze at will. She made sure that he drank milk, not as a food substitute but as part of the meal, and made sure to offer it at the end of the meal, after he'd eaten some solid food. These simple yet consistently implemented changes meant that that Jared was often hungry enough to eat when she put him into the high chair.

If he really fussed at being stuck in the chair, she appropriately interpreted his behavior as a sign that he wasn't quite ready for a meal. So she took him down and let him play for fifteen minutes or so before trying to feed him again. Eventually, he came to associate being in the high chair with the pleasure of eating, instead of the discomfort of being confined. "I think that knowing he wasn't trapped if he didn't want to eat—that he could choose to get down—made a difference," she told me. Having the choice empowered him, and limiting his ability to exercise that choice let Lois get food into him.

Family meals have the added benefit of stimulating children's interest in what and the way you eat. A child who uses a sippy cup will notice you drinking from a regular glass and grow eager to try it. If your child mostly eats with his fingers, he'll want to try using utensils as you do—ready or not. Though most kids don't become truly proficient with a fork and spoon until they're about two or three years old, they may still enjoy practicing with their own small utensils (ergonomic, child-sized versions are available these days). You can have them choose the one they want to use, to make the experience even more satisfying—and the lesson in feeding themselves more indelible.

As for taking an interest in what you eat, consider my experience. Like many new parents, I initially fed my daughter the usual chicken nuggets and other bland finger foods. But once she was old enough to eat with us, she began to lose interest in kiddie fare. She insisted on eating the food we had on our plates—chicken curry, as it turned out, on the first night. She loved it. Food doesn't have to be spice-free for kids to enjoy it, and their hardwired drive to copy grownups is a powerful force to enlist in the fight to broaden and improve their diets. My husband and I were delighted!

Broadening the toddler diet is a concern for many parents. Toddlers often go on streaks of eating only certain foods, even if they're not constant snackers like Jared. The goal is to have the toddler eat something from each of the five major food groups—dairy, protein, carbohydrates, vegetables, and fruit. That can often seem like more of an ideal than a reality.

> Rick was frustrated with eighteen-month-old Miles. "He has jags of eating nothing but breakfast. He seems really hungry, wolfing down fruit, cereal, and toast, then for the rest of the day he barely nibbles. Sometimes the nanny will get him to have some yogurt for a snack, but that's it. Though his favorite dinner is lemon chicken, there are days when he won't even touch it. We've tried making things he's loved in the past, but he'll turn up his nose at whatever is served or maybe just grab a piece of bread. It's like he'll eat nothing but carbs for a couple of days."

Since Miles was healthy and growing and developing well, I assured Rick that his eating habits were not unusual. Many toddlers are erratic diners, going through periods when they focus on certain foods or skip meals altogether. The important thing was to continue to offer Miles a choice of healthy options three times a day, plus a couple of wholesome snacks. Often, to parents' surprise, when toddlers are presented with choices, their diets tend to balance out over time, as Miles's did.

The key is to avoid engaging in a power struggle over food in which every meal becomes a battle. Eating is supposed to be a pleasurable experience, not an upsetting one. Keep it peaceful.

Sometimes, no matter how calm a parent remains, the child is determined to do battle. This was the case with two-year-old Ella.

> "I think I'm doing everything right," said Ella's mother, Andrea. "Ella knows how to feed herself, but now when I put her in the high chair, she just throws her food on the floor. We're trying the family meal approach, but she doesn't seem too interested in watching or engaging with us. She thinks it's more fun to see us jump when she throws food and makes a big mess."
>
> "How do you react?" I asked.
>
> "Well, I try not to react much at all. I just bring out more food without comment. But she throws that too. To be honest, sometimes I just feed her myself to keep mealtime from being a struggle."
>
> "That's certainly understandable," I said. "But, of course, when you feed her or leap from the table, you're giving her loads of attention, which she obviously loves."
>
> "I know that," Andrea said. "I guess I feel outsmarted. I just don't know what else to do to get her to eat."

It's a rare parent who hasn't felt outsmarted by a toddler at some point. My recommendation for Andrea was simple: just take away Ella's plate. I told her to explain why calmly—that food is to eat, not to throw—and not to give back the plate right away when Ella protested. A good rule of thumb when removing misused items is to withhold them for a minute per year of the child's age. For Ella, that meant two minutes of waiting every time she threw her food. By removing the plate, Andrea was giving Ella control, allowing her to choose to eat dinner. But if Ella made the wrong choice, to throw food, that choice would have a consequence, waiting.

Consistency is the key to persuasion. If you're going to take something away from a child, especially one just starting to understand the word *no*, you have to do it for each infraction. If you can't throw food on Monday, you can't get away it with on Tuesday either. If parents stick to their guns, kids do get the message fairly quickly. It took only a few removals over a couple of days for Ella to realize that Andrea meant business and that dinner wasn't playtime.

Parents often worry that toddlers will never learn to sit at the table and eat, that they'll never feed themselves, that they'll never eat balanced meals, that they'll go hungry, and so on. But fear not, these dire predictions virtually never come true. The best way to get through the toddler years is with patience, humor, and delight at the marvel of your growing, changing child. However, any specific concerns that you have should be addressed with your pediatrician.

The Post-Toddler Repast

Offering a range of healthy food choices in toddlerhood is important to establish a baseline of good habits. In the pre-school years and beyond, those habits will be challenged as children become more vocal about their preferences. What's more, as they spend time out of the house or in front of the television, they're inevitably exposed to the sugary, fatty, salty fare that is the unfortunate mainstay of the American diet. We all know the consequences of that diet—an epidemic of obesity as well as serious illnesses such as diabetes. What's most important to realize is that your child's eating habits at this young age are a setup for his future health. Legend has it that, by nature, preschoolers and kindergartners are impossibly fussy eaters. It's become a truism that all they want is white food—French fries, chicken nuggets, rice, and mac and cheese. Entire cookbooks are devoted to sneaking vegetables into "kid" fare to help parents who are losing the nutrition wars. It seems that a whole generation of parents has become short-order cooks to cater to children who balk at eating what's on the dinner table.

Is this necessary? Our own parents certainly didn't think so. Punishments like sending to kids to bed without dinner were the norm but are out of step with our more child-sensitive times. Furthermore, such strictness turns mealtimes into nightmares. No one benefits from that level of constant stress. There's a happy medium between fighting over food and total indulgence. The family meal is too important to be undermined by either extreme.

The family meal is the time when parents can model good food choices for their children. Example is the best teacher. Seeing you eat a variety of foods will encourage your kids to try them, a chance they'll miss out on if you cook them custom "kiddie" meals. Studies show that it may take ten to fifteen tastes before a child will either come to like or definitely dislike a certain food.[2] So be patient, and keep exposing them to different options. It's progress even if one bite is all that a child will accept.

The advantage of having a preschooler/kindergartner over a toddler is that she can meet you halfway between outright refusal and eating what you think she should. For example, children love to dip, so you can say, "I'd like you to try a green pepper. If you don't want it plain, what do you think would make it taste good? Do you want to try it with ranch dressing? With hummus?" Or if you've made black bean chili, you can offer her some cheese to sprinkle on top, if she thinks that would make it more appealing.

Once she's made the decision to accept the ranch dressing or the cheese, she's pretty much committed to trying the food. Which is what you want, but you haven't forced her to eat it. You've given her the responsibility to figure out a way (with your guidance) to get it down. Maybe she won't like it. We all have foods that we simply don't like (or outright can't stand). But by letting her define the conditions, you're making it her independent choice to try the food. As I often tell my own children, "I can only offer you food. I won't force it on you. It's your job to taste it and choose whether to eat it."

Some kids come up with creative ways to do their "job" and taste suspect foods.

Just before Halloween, I suggested the dipping idea to Judith, the mother of my four-year-old patient Mark, as a way to get him to eat vegetables. Rather than fight with him, I urged her to let him decide what would make him want to try them. When she called me a few days later, she was laughing. "Well, I tried him on carrots, but he didn't decide to dip them," she said. "You won't believe what he told me. He said that they looked like skeleton fingers."

"Really?" I asked. "Was that a good or bad thing?"

"It was good," she said. "He stuck a carrot stick in a black olive, which he said was the skeleton's fingernail.

Then he actually ate the whole thing. Can you imagine? That made it fun for him."

As a mother and a pediatrician, I've come to see that along with the power of choice, there's another potent force to draw on when encouraging kids to eat well: their sense of pride. In fact, one of my inspirations for this book was a visit to my own kids' Montessori school. The students, who were no more than three or four, were washing vegetables. When they were done, they sat down to eat the salad they'd made together. Surely there were some picky eaters in that class, but they all seemed to enjoy the salad, thrilled by their accomplishment.

Choosing and Preparing Foods: How to Involve Your Child

I often tell that story when parents complain about their picky-eater preschoolers and kindergartners. A preschooler or kindergartner is old enough to help with food planning and preparation. She'll most likely enjoy doing it and will take great satisfaction from what she achieves. I saw this in my own household when my first-born child was approaching preschool age. Let me share with you what happened:

> One morning when my daughter was three years old, she came into the kitchen while I was busy unloading the dishwasher. Since she wanted breakfast, I suggested that she get started by taking out the supplies. We had moved her cups and bowls to a child-level shelf, so she could pick the ones to use for each meal. The cereal was in a lower cabinet, too. After she chose her cereal, bowl, and spoon, she asked me for the milk. When I turned my back to

go to the fridge, she was already pouring the cereal into her bowl.

Then she asked if she could pour the milk. Though she'd done a pretty good job with the cereal, a big milk carton seemed more challenging. But, hey, she deserved the chance. So I poured some milk out into a measuring cup. That worked perfectly.

Voilà, she'd just made her own breakfast!

Imagine a little person, just three years old, making her own breakfast. She was even more thrilled than I was. From then on, I kept a measuring cup full of milk in the refrigerator door. That was just the first of many meals my kids have prepared themselves.

With supervision, even relatively young children can cook. They make omelets, and my daughter at age eight went through a phase of sautéing bok choy (with close supervision, of course). My son wanted to eat it because his sister made it, and he loved it. Being so competent at such a grownup activity has made them bloom with confidence.

So I strongly encourage the parents of picky preschoolers to involve their children in choosing and preparing food. Here are some strategies that I suggest:

- **Take Your Child to Get Groceries.** Take your child with you to the supermarket. When you're in the produce section, say, have her pick out something green. She may think she doesn't like greens, but if she gets to choose one, she's much more likely to try it. Encourage her to suggest foods in each department. She may not be up for making a decision every time, but you'll have shown her that she is in control of some of the choices.

- **Look for Food Ideas Together.** Watch one of the food channels or flip through a food magazine with your child. Have her think about which dishes look good and pick one out (ideally, not a dessert). Get the ingredients and then make the dish together.

- **Check Out Websites Together.** Look at some healthy kid-friendly food websites with your child. One in particular I like is www.choosemyplate.gov. These sites offer clever everyday ideas, like snacks in the shapes of bugs or sandwiches with funny faces, as well as special holiday-themed offerings, like Father's Day cucumber boats, filled with tuna salad. Your child is sure to find something that she'd enjoy making that looks like it would be fun to eat.

- **Make a Cookbook.** Have your child make a "cookbook," drawing pictures of foods that she likes, foods that she doesn't like, and—importantly—foods that she plans to try. Every so often, have her pick one of the "foods to try" for you to make.

- **Have Your Child Plan a Meal.** Put your child in charge of one family meal during the week, letting her decide what you'll have. Be prepared for some odd combinations, like spaghetti and mashed potatoes. The deal is that she gets to be the boss that night, and on your nights, she'll eat what you want.

- **Plant a Garden.** Plant a garden and let your child choose the seeds she wants to nurture. Whatever she's grown herself, she'll proudly eat.

These are just a few ideas, and I think you'll be surprised at what a difference they can make in your child's approach to food. Instead of feeling like a victim, compelled to choke down food she hates, she'll start feeling like a valued participant in family meals. Having a say will give her a new self-assurance—and, ideally, at least a slightly more expansive view of what she's willing to eat.

Of course, there will still be nights when your child hates something (or on occasion, everything) on her plate. As long as she's willing to try whatever's being served, you should honor those dislikes. But I wouldn't interrupt the meal to jump up and cook her something special. If she rejects what's being offered, she can embrace the responsibility to choose something else, with your guidance. If she's an older kindergarten-aged child and can understand the food groups, you might ask, "Okay, if you don't like the meat, what are you going to have for your protein? Will it be yogurt? Peanut butter? Microwave ravioli?"

If a child is too young to grasp that concept, you can still say, "Okay, go to the fridge and pick out something healthy. It can be cheese, it can be yogurt. . . . It just can't be pudding or cake." By allowing your child to make the choice, you're showing her that she is in control and that there is no need for a food fight.

The goal of this chapter is to take the stress out of mealtimes, when kids often tend to really dig in their heels. The sooner you can instill in them the responsibility to make good choices, the more you will avoid conflict, enjoy peaceful mealtimes, and have well-nourished children.

The Food Fight Recap

Here are some at-a-glance guidelines for sparking kids' interest in food at various ages by nurturing their independence.

- **Birth to Three Months.** The AAP recommends breast feeding exclusively for the first six months of a child's life, offering breast milk along with solid foods from six to twelve months old, then breast feeding as long thereafter as mutually desired by mother and child.[3] Once breastfeeding has been well established, parents can offer breast milk (or formula) in a bottle. At three months, start encouraging your baby to hold his own bottle.

- **Three to Six Months.** If necessary, help the bottle-holding process by curling his hands around the bottle. To avoid choking, never prop up a bottle near him. Always keep your eyes on him during feeding. Keep snuggling, even if not breast feeding, during feeding times.

- **Four to Six Months.** When he has good head control and shows interest in the food others are eating, introduce solid food. Most parents begin with single-grain cereal mixed with formula or breast milk to the consistency of yogurt, although you can begin with fruit or vegetables if you prefer. Give him a tablespoonful at one feeding, in tiny bites, and see what happens. He may grimace initially, because he's adjusting to the texture and learning to swallow. As he begins to master eating, you can increase the amount at each meal.

Gradually increase the number of feedings to two or three per day. Most children will turn away from the spoon when no longer hungry for food.

- **Six to Eight Months.** Your child can try any well-pureed solid food that does not contain honey. Avoid gluey foods like peanut butter or thick purees that can choke him. Introduce a sippy cup, filled with breast milk or formula. If he tries to feed himself, give him his own little spoon and help him to maneuver it.

- **Eight to Ten Months.** He may be ready for finger foods like soft peas and thin strips of toast. Avoid foods that can choke him, like carrots and other hard vegetables. Sprinkle a few small, soft morsels—cooked peas, well-chopped bananas, or puffs that dissolve in his mouth—on the high-chair tray to give him practice at picking them up.

- **Twelve to Sixteen Months.** Wean him off the bottle. Begin by cutting out the nighttime bottle. Gently encourage him to self-feed, if not yet doing so. Demonstrate eating: load a spoon and guide it to his mouth, and pincer his fingers around a small morsel to show how to pick it up. Offer the sippy cup alongside of the meal initially, but if your child is feigning eating, reserve it for the end of the meal. Praise lavishly when self-feeding finally occurs.

- **One to Three Years.** Expect a certain upheaval in eating habits during toddlerhood due to an effort to exert control and the thrill of discovery, which makes it hard for toddlers to settle down. Resist your toddler's determination to fill up on milk and snack foods. Seat him at the family table, even if it means letting him get up to run off a few times. To be sure he consumes food from all of the food groups, present a range of healthy options and lead by example. Avoid power struggles over food. Do your best to keep mealtimes positive, enjoyable, and stress free. Remember, all you can do is offer the food—it's up to your toddler to eat it.

- **Three to Six Years.** Involve your child in grocery shopping, menu planning, and meal preparation. Offer dips—ranch dressing, hummus, you name it—to help the green peppers, carrots, and even broccoli and cauliflower go down. Check out cooking shows, culinary magazines, and children's food websites with your kids to inspire menu choices and fun food presentations. Make healthy eating fun and lay the groundwork for good life habits.

CHAPTER 4

The Potty Police: Toilet Training

Philip, a new patient, seemed upset. He was in my office with his mother, Patrice, who was telling me that he had a problem. "He's two and a half, and we got him into a great preschool, but he needs to be toilet trained to go." she said. "School starts in a couple months. I'm worried that he's not going to make it."

I smiled at Philip, trying to put him at ease, while Patrice kept talking.

"When he was two, we got him a little potty chair that's also a step stool. He would sit on the potty and often not do anything. Then, after watching his daddy, he would sometimes stand on the stool and pee in the big toilet, so I know that he knows how. But he doesn't do that very often, even though now I've got him in training pants to make it easy. He just wets his pants.

"When he was in diapers, he would often tell us when he was pooping. Not these days. I keep reminding him to let me know, so I can put him on the potty. But he won't. Then he gets mad when I clean him up and tell him about the potty again.

"It's like the whole toilet-training thing has become a big drama. My sister has twin girls who were both toilet-trained by age two. She started when they were eighteen months. She says that I missed the training window."

As I listened to Patrice, I reflected on a similar conversation I'd had just that morning.

Dolores was on mission to toilet train two-year-old Jenny. She'd been reading a lot about different methods and was eager to give them a try. "I used to put her on the potty at timed intervals after eating and drinking. But I didn't always catch her before she peed or pooped. So now I stick her on the potty every forty-five minutes, giving her ten minutes to read a book or watch a DVD while she tries to go. Do you think this is a good idea?

"Or would it be better to try that boot-camp thing, when you take the whole weekend and let her run around naked? Then, when she uses the potty, you give her one piece of candy for peeing and two for pooping, like positive reinforcement."

Toilet training—when and how to do it—is one of the hottest discussion topics in my pediatric office. When I hear stories from parents like Patrice and Dolores, all I can say is "Why?" No one likes changing diapers, of course, but why subject your child, not to mention yourself, to the anxiety of making a huge developmental breakthrough by an arbitrary deadline?

Throughout this book, I've stressed encouraging children to embrace their innate capabilities at appropriate stages. But when it comes to toilet training, when the appropriate stage is different for each child, a lot of parents seem to spring into over-achiever mode. Sometimes I feel like asking, "Is there a Potty Prize, like an Olympic medal, for the first kid who's out of diapers? What's the rush?"

Typically, somewhere between eighteen months and three and a half years, most children will have some interest in transitioning from diapers to underwear. This is a very wide range, which should be comforting to parents. If you have a four-year-old who still shows no interest, it's a good idea to check in with your pediatrician to make sure there isn't an underlying reason, but most times that child will wake up one day and decide it's time to use the potty.

Of course, like Patrice, many parents are pushed to accomplish toilet training by a school, camp, or day-care requirement. I had that experience myself when I was considering sending my then two-and-a-half-year-old to summer camp with his sister. Since we'd planned a family vacation in the spring, staying in our own cottage with my sister and her family, I figured that I might as well try to toilet train him then.

When we got to the cottage, I set up a little potty chair outdoors. To remove any obstacles, I let my son go diaper-free. Then I asked my daughter and nephew to use the outdoor potty, so my son could see them and want to act like "one of the kids."

They were thrilled. Since my son was running around without clothes, they insisted on going naked as well. A naked vacation? An outdoor toilet? That was their idea of heaven!

But even their glee wasn't enough to sway my son. My daughter and nephew used the potty, but he peed and pooped everywhere but there. Finally, I had to concede that my plan wasn't working. So, okay—he wouldn't be going to camp with his sister that summer. Life went on . . .

Before long, he became inspired to try using the potty, and then it was a breeze to get him toilet trained. I followed his timetable, and by the time he was four, he was dry day and night.

We've all heard of children who are diaper-free at eighteen months and of those who are not fully toilet trained, daytime and nighttime (which are often mastered separately with nighttime often taking longer), until age six. This normal range of ages is so wide because bladder and bowel control are complicated, requiring cognitive and emotional development as well as physical skills. The fact that your child, at a given age, hasn't yet assembled all those pieces of the puzzle is no reflection on her intelligence. She is, most likely, just not ready.

Philip clearly wasn't ready. Occasionally mimicking his father was not a sign that he was willing to use the toilet on a regular basis. Toilet training had become, in Patrice's words, a "drama" because Philip was frustrated at being expected to perform a function before he was motivated to do it. No doubt he wanted to please Patrice, and her reprimands when he soiled his pants had him confused and upset.

If a child-care facility, school, or camp makes toilet training a condition of attendance, I suggest that you ask the caregivers if they are willing and/or able to work with you and your child. For example, you can say something like "This is not a process that I can control. Ultimately, it's up to my child to decide when she is ready. I imagine that seeing the other children in her class use the bathroom will be inspiring for her and she will be trained in no time at all." You may also want to ask if there is anything that you can do as a parent to make it easier on the teachers. Trust me, you are not the only parent who finds that toilet training can rarely be accomplished on demand. If the institution is unable or unwilling to offer any flexibility on their policy, you may need to ask yourself whether it's the right place at that particular time for your child.

Patrice's chosen school was willing to accommodate Philip, suggesting that he wear training pants (commonly referred to as pull-ups) to make it easier for teachers to change him. And, as is often the case, simply being surrounded by children who were a little farther along in their toilet training efforts helped motivate Philip. He soon got the hang of it, as all kids eventually do.

As for Dolores, she believed, like many parents, that toilet training is just a matter of finding the right formula. There are countless strategies to try, and most of their promoters promise instant success. But cycling through these schemes, one after another, may subject your child to repeated rounds of failure and months of struggle. The truth is, there is no magic gimmick that you can expect to work. Toilet training is not something that you can simply impose on your child.

If you give your child the space to choose when she wants to be toilet trained and what will help her independently achieve it, she's much more likely to have a smoother passage through this transition to maturity.

All in Good Time

Toilet training is the process of giving your child responsibility for his own body. Think about what that responsibility entails: being able to sense when he needs to go, having the foresight to know what will happen if he misses his body's cues, being able to "hold it" long enough to reach the bathroom, understanding the point of the toilet, being able to aim eliminations into it, and so on. All of these are internal processes that only he can coordinate. You can't possibly instill any of these abilities in him. Only time will help him develop them.

That's why, despite Patrice's sister's theory, there is no one particular age, like eighteen months, that presents a "window" for toilet training. Children's interest in the process often ebbs and flows. At eighteen months, a child may or may not be physically able to sense the urge to go. Even if he can tell, he may not yet be motivated to make the effort to use the potty. He may not yet really connect the feeling of having to go with the actual excretion process. He may be entering the rebellious toddler phase, resisting being put on the potty to assert control. And he may not yet have the verbal skills to fully understand directions, to comfortably express the need to go, or to articulate any fears or worries about the process. While he may be interested in seeing adults or older kids use the toilet, like my son on vacation, he may have not figured how, exactly, to imitate them or even if he wants to imitate them. Or he simply doesn't have any interest in imitating what he sees. These are just a few age-appropriate reasons why, at any given time, toilet training may not click for a child.

So the best approach is to lay the groundwork and let your child take the lead. If you like, you can initiate the concept (like buying a potty and reading books on the subject) as early as eighteen months. This means you can introduce them to the "tools of the trade," but be sure not to use pressure or have expectations. There's a difference between introducing the language and actually initiating the process. If you cannot resist, you may be in for a lengthy wait. Research shows that the sooner you start toilet training, the longer the process will take.

One study on toilet training defined "initiating training" as setting up a potty chair and explaining it to the child; asking the child three or more times a day if he had to go was considered "intensive training." Interestingly, the kids who first encountered the potty at eighteen months (but were not asked about it repeatedly) stayed dry in the daytime sooner than others, while those who began "intensive training" early on did not reach this milestone any more quickly. So, while you may want to introduce your child to the concept of the toilet, becoming the "potty police" by constantly asking if he needs to go, will not speed up the process. In fact, the researchers saw little benefit in starting "intensive training" in children under twenty-seven months old.[1]

That's not to say that twenty-seven months is the golden age of toilet training. The authors of the study specifically warn against that conclusion and instead recommend that you begin actual training, opposed to merely introducing the potty, when your child seems ready.

On Your Mark. . . .

But how can you judge readiness? First, consider whether your child has reached the following developmental milestones:

- **She can walk well.** A child who learns to walk at, say, one year of age, will probably be too wobbly for at least the first few months to focus on exploring another new skill. By eighteen to twenty-four months, she will likely be more open to expanding her repertoire of grown-up activities like toilet training.

- **She can pull down her pants and underpants by herself.** For a while, she may need help undressing to use the toilet, but being able to deal with taking off and pulling on her clothing is a sign of motor skill refinement. This useful potty training (not to mention life) skill usually kicks in at around eighteen months. That said, at the outset of toilet training, it's good to dress kids in easy-off/easy-on outfits, without lots of layers, buckles, or belts that stand in the way.

- **She can sit still long enough to use the potty.** It helps to keep in mind that young children tend to sit still longer if you engage them in activities like looking at pictures in a book that can keep their attention (and them) from wandering.

- **She indicates awareness that she is going to (or needs to) use the bathroom,** like pulling at a dampening diaper or squatting and/or hiding.

As she masters the physical requirements for successful potty training, you should also be on the lookout for more cognitive/emotional signs of readiness:

- **She demonstrates the ability to plan and solve problems.** For example, if she's between twelve and eighteen months old, she'll recognize that she can follow you when you leave the room. This capacity, which grows more sophisticated by age two and beyond, will help her picture the potty as the solution to having to go, even when it's not immediately in front of her.

- **She remembers things,** including where the potty is and her experiences using it.

- **She's developing focus,** the capacity to aim for a goal without getting waylaid by distractions.

- **She plays imaginatively** and can act out potty scenarios with animals and dolls.

- **She enjoys sitting on or talking about the potty** rather than seeming fearful about the process.

- **She becomes interested in other people's toilet habits.**

Get Set. . . .

When your child starts to display these signs of readiness—usually between eighteen and thirty months old—you can read books and watch videos about toilet training with him.[2] When you change his diapers, you can talk about how good it feels to be clean and dry, as your goal is to emphasize the positive, even when he uses his diaper rather than the potty. Have a same-sex adult take the child into the bathroom to demonstrate what to do (with the understanding that it's easier for some boys just learning to use the toilet to sit down for both functions; when they get more accomplished, they can stand up to urinate). Set up a potty chair that he can practice sitting on, clothed or unclothed. It's also good to familiarize him with a portable insert that fits over the regular toilet seat. I find this type useful because you can throw it in a bag and take it with you when you go out.

You can begin talking about using the potty as a new adventure, but let your child decide when he wants to actually try it. The idea of trying to acclimate a probably-too-young child by plopping him on the toilet, as Dolores did, and making him sit there until he poops or pees, doesn't make sense to me. It's too frustrating for a toddler to be pinned down, and besides, at best it establishes the toilet as a place where nothing happens. At worst, it can come off as punishment and a cause for rebellion. Instead, wait until he gives you cues, such as

- Telling you that he needs a diaper change
- Telling you that he needs to go
- Expressing interest in trying the potty
- Asking to wear underwear

Further, if he's started having bowel movements at regular intervals and can stay dry in a diaper for two straight hours, he may be primed to begin.

Go!

A child who's decided that she's ready for toilet training is self-motivated. You want to maintain that motivation by keeping the experience upbeat and reassuring, as self-motivation is the key ingredient for potty-training success. Ideally, she'll be able to tell you when she needs to go (or she may tell you nonverbally, by jumping up and down, hiding, squirming, or clutching herself). Her timing won't give you a lot of leeway, so be prepared to drop everything in order to help her more quickly get settled on the potty. Be sure to praise her each time she tells you she has to go, whether or not she follows through or makes it in time.

In my experience, it can be very productive to reward children for the accomplishment of actually making it to the toilet on time. Some toilet-training gurus suggest using small candies as rewards for successful toilet trips. I personally prefer not to use food as a reward. In my own home, for both of my children, we used a chart made of foam-core with a ladder drawn on it. When my children were working toward a certain behavioral goal, they would get to put a sticker on the chart for each time goals were successfully achieved. As the achievements mount, the clusters of stickers rise toward the top of the ladder, which is very exciting for a child. Seeing all those stickers as a visual record and collective reminder of the many small triumphs they represent can be tremendously motivating.

In the beginning, you might want to use small stickers or foil stars for each successful toilet experience. Then have your child "graduate" to using larger stickers to mark dry days.

And when a child doesn't make it or has an accident? It's best to simply be matter of fact. Just assure your child she'll have plenty of chances to try again. Making a fuss about the misjudgment or accident can leave children feeling overly scrutinized and self-conscious. Be sure that anyone else who cares for your child—whether it's a nanny, a child-care provider, or a grandparent—is fully on board with this "reward or ignore" potty policy. The important end result is that everyone involved works together to acknowledge your child's potty-training successes and overlooks any inevitable missteps.

Scolding or punishing a child for accidents is not only demotivating but likely to spark rebellion. Worse, it can have very unpleasant physical effects. I sometimes treat kids with encoporesis, a miserable state of constipation that can be caused by (among other things) fear of using the toilet for bowel movements. Regardless of the initial cause, stool gets so backed up and hard that kids with encopresis come to hate even trying to move their bowels because it hurts. As their systems get increasingly backed up, poop leaks out around the hard, compacted stuck stool. It's a treatable condition, but one that I would far rather prevent from occurring in the first place.

Once your child has accumulated a little string of successes, she can move up to the grand prize—shedding her diapers for underpants. Mark this major passage with a drum roll! Let her pick out the underpants she'd like to try, maybe ones depicting superheroes or other favorite and frequently coveted designs.

Underpants are both more motivating and more of a learning tool for the child than intermediate steps like training pants. With underpants, it's clear when an accident has occurred, and avoiding that damp, wet feeling generally proves to be a big incentive for the child.

Today's disposable diapers and training pants are designed to keep pee and poop in, while keeping kids comfortable. The problem is they are so effectively absorbent that a child wearing them often has trouble recognizing that she's wet. So, if you want to use training pants because they're easier to change, go ahead. Just don't think of them as anything but diapers.

The other thing I routinely suggest to facilitate a more successful transition is that once you commit to putting your child in underpants, stick with it. For example, don't just reach for a diaper for your child for a long ride in the car. Switching back and forth between underpants and diapers will usually prove too confusing for your child. You have to make the same commitment to underpants that your child has made, which can mean stopping to find a bathroom or using a portable potty seat. However, here are some exceptions to a no-diaper policy, as the Potty Reset sidebar shows.

For some children, urinating in the potty is easy, but there's a disconnect when it comes to defecation. That was the situation that Don described when he came to my office with three-and-half-year-old Allie.

"She seems to like wearing underpants," he said. "She has some cute ones with butterflies. But when she has to move her bowels, she asks for a diaper instead of using the potty. We let her use the diaper, but then when we try to flush the poop down the toilet, she gets upset.

"Yesterday she didn't even mention that she had to poop. When I went into her room, where she was playing, she had a funny look on her face. There was a smell in the air, so I looked around. There, behind the chair, I found it. She'd pooped on the floor. I'm worried that there's something really wrong with her."

Odd as this behavior may seem to civilized adults, it makes perfect sense in the toddler realm. It may reflect a child who is

Potty Reset

There are two common predicaments that may cause you to legitimately hit the "reset" button on toilet training. The first is when the process is simply not working, and the second is when it has stopped working. In both cases, it can be very helpful to consult your pediatrician to be sure that there's no physical reason for the issue. Once that worry is out of the way, the reset method for both predicaments is the same: *act like it's not a big deal.*

Predicament 1. Toilet training has become a power struggle with you coaxing, begging, scolding, and even trying to bribe your child to use the potty, but to no avail. As we've noted in earlier chapters, toddlers are notoriously headstrong, excited about using their newfound powers to impose their will on the world. The stress of the struggle isn't at all likely to improve the situation, so just remove the stress. It's time to back off, to take yourself out of the equation. Ask yourself, What am I gaining here?

Stepping back is not the same as giving up. It's a proactive strategy to give your child the space and time to realize that he really doesn't want to spend the rest of his life in diapers. Remember that he is the only one who will ever be able to physically sense that he needs to go, and that self-motivation is the ultimate secret to success. That means that only he can assume the responsibility for toilet training. Let have him have that responsibility, and it will happen.

simply too slow to respond to the urge to go, be a result of defiance, or even be a sign of anxiety about some aspect of toilet training, like fear of being whirled down the potty with her poop or of that scary flushing sound the toilet makes. Whatever the cause, in the vast majority of cases, this stage fortunately

Predicament 2. Your child has graduated to underpants and then suddenly he regresses and starts having accidents, even in the daytime. The first thing to do is schedule a visit to your pediatrician to make sure the accidents aren't the result of a urinary tract infection or other medical explanation. Once you have determined that's not the case, you can consider behavioral causes. Maybe you've just had a new baby, or maybe your child is overly excited or nervous about starting preschool or kindergarten. Whatever the reason, this is not the time to pressure your child about toilet training, reminding him that he is a big boy, and so on.

It's more productive to say, "It doesn't seem like you're ready to be in underpants right now. That's fine; it's perfectly okay. Would you rather be in diapers at the moment? If that's your choice, let's do it."

Stay neutral, with no hint of recrimination or talk of "going back to diapers," which can make your child feel like he's losing something. Just remove the stress.

If you act like don't care, you're leaving it up your child to decide when he's ready to start or resume using the toilet. And when you think about it, why should you care? Sure, changing diapers can be a pain, but if you have a toddler or preschooler, you must be used to it. Looking at the big picture, what bearing can being toilet trained a month or two later possibly have on your child's future? No high school, college, or employer will ever ask, "When exactly were you toilet trained?"

passes fairly quickly—in a couple of weeks or a month—as children's urination and defecation habits fall into place, especially when there's no pressure from parents to do it "their" way.

I urged Don to handle situations like his daughter's poop-behind-the-couch episode calmly. Reacting with disgust or shaming a child is never productive (much less kind). It is far better—and far more likely to resolve the behavior—if you ask your child, in a supportive way, what will help her ask for a diaper or, better yet, use the potty. She may not be able to articulate exactly what's wrong, but she may offer you enough insight to brainstorm a solution with her.

In Allie's case, that turned out to be putting the contents of the diaper into the small potty, then letting her dump it into the big toilet herself. Don would leave it there, waiting to flush the toilet until after Allie left the bathroom. The sound of flushing and the sight of the poop swirling down the toilet had her frightened, as if she herself could be flushed away. A grownup toilet can look awfully big and menacing to a child.

It only took a week or two before Allie was able to use the adult potty and get over her fear of the flushing sound.

Nighttime May Not Yet Be the Right Time

Many kids achieve dryness in the daytime long before they master it at night. When your child "graduates" to underpants, you'll want to use them in the daytime, when you or a caretaker can offer encouragement and help. But at night, bladder control, in particular, can be much harder for some children to manage.

This can be understandably worrisome to many parents. In fact, some of the most common questions I get about toilet training relate to nighttime dryness (or rather, the lack of it).

At four going on five, Charley was already into basketball. He went to a basketball clinic on weekends, held in the nearby school gym. He loved watching games on TV with his dad, who was thinking of surprising him with a trip to a professional game for his birthday. His mother, Ilene, loved the idea but wondered if she should try to kill two birds with one stone, by making such a special treat contingent on his staying dry all night.

"He's perfectly fine all day," she told me. "He's been in underpants for months now, with barely an accident. Even when he takes naps, he's okay. But at night, he just pees without waking up. It's like he sleeps too soundly or something.

"So, do you think if I told him that he'd get a really great surprise, it would motivate him to stop peeing at night? I just don't know what else I could offer that would work. We've already tried giving him stickers to reward him for dry nights, but that's not working."

"It sounds like he isn't developmentally ready to be dry at night," I said. "You don't want to make him feel bad and discouraged if he doesn't manage it. That basketball game sounds like too important an event for him and your husband to make it contingent on his nighttime dryness. At his age, it's not a question of motivation. If he's peeing at night, he probably can't help it."

By one estimate from the American Academy of Pediatrics (AAP), 40 percent of children who are fully toilet trained in the daytime continue to wet their pants at night for months, or even a year or two.[3] Under the age of six, many children are unable to sense when they need to urinate at night. The problem is often a matter of biology, plain and simple. If and when it's not matter of will for the child, then there's no incentive parents can offer that will do any good.

It can help, however, to restrict drinks after 5:00 p.m. and make sure that he stops in the bathroom on his way to bed. But the main thing is to stay calm and not stress yourself or your child about nighttime accidents. Conflict can only worsen the situation. And why make your child feel bad about himself?

It's always wise to consult your pediatrician with any worries about your child's toilet training. But for nighttime peeing, once you've ascertained that your toddler or preschooler is healthy, the answer is often easy: let him in sleep in diapers or training pants until he's ready to make the switch.

Remember, the point of toilet training is transferring responsibility for the workings of his own body to the child. He's the only one who can assume that responsibility. You can't wake up and pee for him. He has to do that independently. If you wake him up to pee, you'll both miss out on sleep. So the best thing to do is wait for his body and mind to mature enough to get the message.

As I said to Ilene, "Who cares what Charley sleeps in? If he's still having accidents at six or seven, we'll talk. But I think probably he'll get the hang of nighttime toilet training before that. A majority of kids do.

"So don't worry. I've never seen a kid get married in diapers yet!"

The Potty Police Recap

Here are some at-a-glance rough age parameters for toilet training. But keep in mind that this important milestone will likely not be achieved until a child is independently motivated to attempt it. Let her take the lead.

- **Eighteen to Twenty-Four Months.** The earlier you start toilet training, the longer you can expect it to take. Most kids are not physically, cognitively, and emotionally ready to attempt training until around two to two-and-a-half years old—if then. Set up a potty or read books on toilet training with your child, in case she gets interested, but don't pressure her.

  Hold off on toilet training until the child signals readiness: asking for a diaper change, talking about the urge to go, and expressing interest in the potty or in underwear—as well as staying dry for two hours and having regular bowel movements.

- **Twenty-Four Months On—or When Ready.** A child who's ready will tell you when she needs to go, either in words or by squirming, jumping up and down, and so on. When you get the signal, drop everything and immediately guide your child toward the potty. Offer small nonfood rewards, like foil stars on a chart, for notifying you and larger rewards, like bigger stickers, for dry days. Downplay misjudgments or accidents (never scold!): assure her that she'll have plenty of other chances to make it.

  After several successful days, try for the grand prize: underpants. Keeping underpants dry is a major incentive for the child.

Once your child commits to underpants, ensure that she can reach a bathroom in time. Save diapers for nighttime. Under stress, she may regress. Offer her the choice of using diapers. Make it clear that the choice is totally hers and that you're fine with whatever she decides.

Remember, a child who's comfortable with the potty when it comes to peeing may find pooping more of a challenge. If your child can't articulate what's wrong, talk supportively and helpfully with her to devise a workable plan to deal with her feelings and fears.

- **Three to Six Years.** A child who has mastered daytime toilet training may still need nighttime diapers until age six. It's simply a matter of biology, so let your child sleep in diapers until her mind and body get in sync.

CHAPTER 5

Child's Play:
The Imagination Lab

One warm summer afternoon, I was at a local park with my children and a close friend with kids the same age. As we sat having a picnic, we observed another mother feverishly trying to entertain her seemingly bored five-year-old daughter. "Do you want to go on the swings?" she asked. "How about trying the slide? Do you want to play in the sandbox?"

The child's answer to each question was "No, that's boring!"

Here the two of them were, outside, in a beautiful park with plants in bloom. There were plenty of other kids to meet and interesting contraptions to play on. But this child could not be entertained. Instead, she plopped down on her mother's lap and began to play with her smart phone.

The American Academy of Pediatrics reports that 90 percent of parents regularly expose children under the age of two to electronic media. By the time they become toddlers, kids are watching an average of one to two hours of television per day.[1]

And it's not just TV that's commanding their attention. A recent report from Common Sense Media tracked the profound impact of the digital revolution on children. Among kids two to four years old, 53 percent use computers and 52 percent are familiar with mobile devices, such as smart phones. Fifty-eight percent can play computer games, a number that sadly surpasses the mere 52 percent that can ride bikes. Compare the 19 percent who can work a smart phone app to the number of kids who can tie their shoes (just 11 percent).[2] It's a challenge to reconcile our tech-dependent modern world with children's visceral need for the kind of free, off-screen play that promotes their emotional, cognitive, social, and motor development. It's important to note that digital media is not categorically bad, but we just need to do our best to make sure our children use it wisely and that it doesn't interfere with learning other life skills like riding a bike and playing at a park.

As for structured activities, consider the range of enrichment programs open to children under preschool age: reading and math tutoring; foreign language learning; music and art; sports like swimming, tennis, and soccer; gymnastics; tumbling; yoga; karate; and ballet are just a few of the offerings available in many communities. Parents have trouble resisting these programs, if they can afford them. The academic ones, especially, appeal to parents who worry that their kids will suffer a disadvantage in preschool, lagging behind children who can already read, write, and add.

But consider what Allison Gopnik, a psychology professor, had to say about this in the *New York Times*: "The best you can say [about these programs] is that they're useless." She offered an analogy equating super-early achievers to a species of elks who compete with others by growing huge antlers. "The result is that they go around tottering, unable to walk, under the enormous weight of these antlers they've developed."[3]

That's a scary image. Instead of looking for ways to forge (or force) your child's way to academic success, the key is to find the right balance for your child. There are only so many hours in a day, and you want to leave space for family time and self-directed playtime. Among other attributes, play is instrumental in facilitating the casual, free-flowing interactions that teach kids how to build and conduct human relationships. Just as importantly, we want to allow for children's personal time, when they can explore the world, hatch and test out ideas, and begin to develop a sense of themselves. It's often been said that our children's job—their proper work—is play. So it's critical that we, as parents, should hold play sacrosanct in our children's lives and, whenever possible, offer opportunities for them to dream up and perform activities independently. Creating your own fun is, after all, the cornerstone of imaginative thinking.

Baby Bliss

Play is the primary way that your baby will begin to connect with the world. In the first few months of life, even when he can't move around much, he will probably be fixated on things like mobiles above his head. If you put him on the floor in front of a mirror, he will be captivated by seeing his face and by the reflections of his movements. Around three months of age, when he can hold up his head well enough for tummy time, he'll delight in the toys you put in front of him. By giving him the opportunity to make these independent discoveries, you'll introduce him to the fascinations the world can hold.

The toys you give him can help expand his awareness even more. There's a reason that so many classic baby toys are sensory stimulants—brightly colored, with high-contrast designs to engage the eye; noisy, like rattles (with thrilling sound and motion); pleasing touch because they're textured, fuzzy, fluffy, and even scratchy; chewable; and so on. Babies revel in exploring the powers of their five senses. The actual toy isn't as important as what your child does with it. For example, a wooden spoon and a bowl can make a great musical instrument.

Other great baby toys invite manipulation and movement—rings to stack on posts, objects to plug into holes, balls to creep after when they roll away. You can stimulate and amuse your baby by, say, lying on the floor a foot or so away from her and letting her try to scooch toward you. When she stares at or reaches for something, don't just hand it over. Let her grab for it on her own (though, obviously, not to the point of frustration). Activities like these help develop motor skills and also encourage problem solving. It is through such active play that your child learns to reason and to understand how her body works.

The AAP discourages any screen exposure at all in the first two years of children's lives—even if children watch programs that are marketed explicitly as "educational." In fact, in a November 2011 policy statement, the AAP cited studies showing that children from eight to sixteen months old with heavy media exposure had expressive language delays, at least in the short term, and heavy media users under a year old had a "significantly higher chance" of speech delays.[4]

Even when the child didn't actually watch the TV, which was kept on for hours as background noise in 39 percent of sampled households, there was still an associated risk. A study of twelve-, twenty-four-, and thirty-six-month-old children showed that background TV distracted them from playing because, when it caught their attention, it broke their concentration and they lost track of their games. TV also reduced their interaction with adults, who, perhaps unconsciously, kept an eye on the screen. Voices emanating from a screen are no substitute for real, human communication, responses to vocalizations that teach a child the emotional color and rhythms of speech.[5]

These are important findings. While the AAP acknowledges that it may be unrealistic to expect parents of children under two to keep their homes media free, it urges them to be conscious of the effects of screen viewing.

Does that mean that you must constantly hold, talk to, and entertain your child? The answer is no. In fact, from the age of four months on, children actually benefit from short stretches of playing on their own—with age-appropriate supervision, of course—so that they can explore and begin to master their environment. They won't get a chance to do that if you're always hovering over them, anticipating and fulfilling every need and desire. Even babies are instinctively curious. As they problem-solve to satisfy their curiosity, they start to develop reasoning powers while building motor skills.

So, when your baby is around three months old, don't hesitate to try putting him down on the floor periodically, with interesting objects to investigate close at hand. Once he can sit up, a whole new universe of playthings—nesting measuring cups, wooden spoons, boxes, and things to hide in them, and so on—will be at his command. When he can crawl, look out! He'll discover wastebaskets worth rummaging through and kitchen cabinets full of fascinating pots and pans.

Needless to say, babies need careful oversight as soon as they begin to make these explorations. It will be fun to watch him and also instructive, showing you what engages him and what skills he's developing and best at. You can then build on these observations when you play with him. Better yet, he'll be making big developmental strides during independent play.

Toddler Tricks

Toddlers have what seems like endless energy, which can be exhausting for many parents. It's very tempting to let them watch television so you can have a bit of downtime or get some chores finished. But this doesn't always have the intended consequence, as evidenced by Tyler's story.

> Two-and-half-year-old Tyler was whiny. He kept trying to get up and down from the chair where his mother, Susan, had installed him as we settled into my consulting room to talk.
>
> Susan lifted him into her lap to try to calm him. Still, he kept squirming and interrupting with "Mommy! Mommy!"
>
> "Do you want a snack, Tyler?" she asked, rifling through her voluminous handbag. "Raisins, juice box, crackers. . . . "
>
> "No!"

"Do you want to look at a book? When she took one out to show him, he batted it out of her hand. He was kicking at her legs, so she put him down.

"No! Up!"

With a big sigh, Susan retrieved the book from the floor and picked him up.

"He's been cranky lately," Susan said, apologetically. "He doesn't seem to sleep well. It's like he has too much energy."

"Does he play outside?" I asked. "Does he do a lot of running around?"

"Yes, we get him outside, but what he really likes is TV."

"Does he watch a lot?"

"Well, we pretty much limit him to the PBS-type kids' programs and videos. He tends to watch it a lot at night because it helps him fall asleep. That's why we have a TV in his room."

In a survey cited in the AAP November 2011 policy statement, 30 percent of the parents who were interviewed responded that television was a sleep aid for their toddlers, and 29 percent of those two- and three-year-olds had TVs in their rooms. At the same time, research has demonstrated that nighttime TV viewing can disrupt sleep habits, especially in children under the age of three.[6] Many parents are shocked when they start to track their kids' (and own) screen hours. Yet these days, when we're all so connected, they really mount up.

Tyler seemed healthy in other respects, so it was certainly possible that his viewing habits were keeping him awake and contributing to his crankiness.

I therefore recommended that Susan remove the TV from his room and start to limit his total screen time (including any time spent on a computer or a similar device) to no more than an hour or two per day. I suggested that she make television viewing not a habit but a special, scheduled activity they did together. Around the age of two, children begin to understand the content of TV programs and, by watching with parents and discussing them, can benefit from their lessons. She could make passive entertainment a more active engagement with Tyler.

But this would be just an initial step toward getting Tyler away from the screen and into critical independent play, not to mention more physically active. The years from one to three are the age when motor skills are starting to coalesce, and children begin climbing, jumping, skipping, catching, and throwing with glee, if not with much skill. It is a major developmental step to master these movements, which may not fully click until around age five, so it was important to get Tyler out to the playground to try his wings. It would help him use up some of that abundant toddler energy.

I could see from the way that Tyler kept trying to get in and out of his chair by himself that he was ready to take on these movement challenges. Susan confirmed that, in the house, he could make it up the stairs, but coming down was still a bit dicey. I encouraged her to let him do it alone, standing close by to catch him if necessary—that is, whenever possible, to create safe situations in which he could experiment.

Tyler was also approaching an age when refined hand and finger skills would let him start cutting paper with blunt child's scissors, drawing, and maybe even copying letters. "Keep his art supplies and other toys on low shelves," I told her, "so he can see play options that might interest him and just help himself."

"I wish I'd thought of that," Susan said. "Right now, it's always, 'Mommy! I need you!' whenever he's bored. I feel like a recreation director, always trying to come up with play ideas."

Any option Tyler chose—and, importantly, even the act of choosing the activity, figuring out how to entertain himself—would be better for him, developmentally speaking, than even the most educational of television or computer programs. The Play Reset sidebar on page 128 offers some strategies to encourage children from toddler age onward to take charge of their own playtime.

Finally, at two and a half, he had cognitive skills to work on in the form of both social and imaginative play. What's especially magical about the toddler years is the child's new capacity to dramatize—to make up stories and create (and assign) roles to play in imagined scenarios. Acting out stories gives the child practice at real-life social interactions. Parents should strongly encourage and participate in such fantasy play, while yielding creative control—the invention and direction of the play—to the child. I told Susan that she could kill two birds with one stone by trying a game I played with my children. We called it Me and Mommy Time. The beauty of Me and Mommy Time was that it was a precious, uninterrupted period when my child and I would be alone in the room and he or she would decide exactly what we would do. Here is an example of how it worked.

> When it was time for Me and Mommy Time, I would announce to my daughter that she was in charge and that she had my full attention. I recall one day in particular, when she decided we were going to play with her puppet theater. She dumped out all of the puppets, and she chose

which puppets each of us played. Initially, she chose a girl for herself, and a fairy godmother for me. I allowed her to develop the entire storyline by frequently asking her what my puppet would do. I was delighted in her imaginative answers. Once when I asked, "What will the fairy godmother do?" She answered, "She'll use her magical powers to give food to the animals." Then, I touched her puppet with my wand and intoned, in my fairy-godmother voice, "Let all of the animals have their favorite foods!" She quickly made a circle of her animal puppets alongside of some of her stuffed animals and pretended to feed them. They gobbled up the pretend food and she giggled.

Then I asked, "Does the fairy godmother stay and eat too?"

"No, she leaves," my daughter replied.

My puppet exited, and I waited to be told which other parts I would play, and what they each would be doing in our story.

The important aspect of this game, apart from being a one-on-one interaction, was that my daughter was the "brains" of our team, creatively developing and completely directing the activity.

Susan loved the idea of the game and thought Tyler would really respond to it, only with superheroes instead of a fairy godmother. I warned her that it might take a little practice for Tyler to get the hang of conducting the play. It wasn't immediately natural for my daughter, who isn't the bossy type, to take charge and dream up the storyline, but she soon got into it, growing more expansive and inventive each time we played. "I think part of the incentive was being able to tell her mother what to do," I told Susan, laughing. "That's real power for a toddler. It's the power of independence!

"And it gave me a bargaining chip: when I wanted her to do something, like pick up her toys, I could say, 'Remember when we played puppets and you were the boss? Now it's my turn to give the orders!'"

This is just one of the countless alternatives to television and computer games that can stretch toddlers' and preschoolers capabilities, helping them to work toward age-appropriate developmental targets. Here is another idea from my family that helps break the cycle of screen dependency. Twice a year, we have screen-free week. During that week, we concentrate on each other—talking, reading together, cooking and baking together, playing board games, doing arts and crafts, and so on. Anything that doesn't involve a TV, computer, or smart phone is fair game. If a week seems too long, try it for a weekend. You'd be surprised at how many great active-entertainment schemes you and your kids can come up with—and how much fun you can have.

The What Independent Play Nurtures sidebar on page 124 lists some of the many skills developed through independent play, while the What Passive Play Prevents sidebar on page 125 lists a few activities that suffer as a result of passive play.

Social interaction and conflict negotiation also begin at this stage when children really connect with others their own age, making friends and learning how to play with them. Parents should be sure to foster these vitally important relationships and, as far as possible, let kids conduct them independently, which will teach them cooperation, sharing, leading and following, communication, and other essential aspects of social interaction.

Post-Toddler Pastimes

In my office, I am seeing more and more children with schedules that rival those of professional athletes. They are always on the go, being shuttled from one organized activity to the next. As a parent, I can understand why. We all want our children to be exposed to a variety of activities, but constantly being on the go has a downside, too.

> "I don't want to go! I don't want to go! I could hear my friend Ellen's son shouting in the background as she picked up the phone.
>
> "Is this a bad time?" I asked.
>
> Ellen chuckled a little. "I'm the one who should be whining. Do I really want to spend my weekend dragging Ian all over town? This morning it's soccer, then there's his math lesson, and at four o'clock he's got a birthday party. I don't even want to think about tomorrow's commitments. He's booked solid!
>
> "I'd let him stay home, but today it's my turn to drive the soccer carpool. Five bickering kids! Even watching DVDs doesn't keep them quiet."

What Independent Play Nurtures

- Imaginative thinking and role playing
- Analytical, logical, and critical thinking
- Communication and cooperation with others (children and adults)
- Face-to-face play (teaching negotiation and conflict resolution)
- Questioning and problem solving

I laughed sympathetically. "Remember when we were kids? Cars didn't have DVD players."

"Yeah, all we could do was spot cars with out-of-state license plates. That, and play Hangman or I Spy."

"Those games were actually pretty entertaining," I said. "And they involved actual skills, like observing and spelling and adding up clues."

Many parents feel like Ellen—that their kids are so over-scheduled that their own lives are on hold. But think about how all those commitments affect their kids. As Ian's complaint highlights, children need downtime too.

Yet there's a lot of peer pressure on both children and parents to make every waking minute count. If all her friends are playing soccer or chess, your child won't want to feel left out. If she's drawn to a musical instrument, how can a parent say no? As for academic enrichment programs, it's usually parents who push children into them, fearing that otherwise they'll enter kindergarten at a disadvantage. Some experts suggest, however, that

What Passive Play Prevents

- **Reading or Being Read To.** The AAP November 2011 Policy Statement cites research showing that children in households where the TV is usually on engage with the written word 25 percent less often (for three- to four-year-olds) and 38 percent less often (for five- to six-year-olds) than kids in homes with low media use. They are less likely to be good readers.[7]

- **Exercising.** According to the AAP, children today are only 25 percent as active as their grandparents were. This has obvious implications for the epidemic obesity in America.[8]

fun, unstructured educational activities, like trips to museums and zoos, may instill a more durable love of learning. They force a child to be creative and take control rather than going along with a teacher's program. In this fast-paced society, knowing how to fill downtime is an important skill for children to learn.

The challenge is to find balance and, most of all, to ensure that your kids have plenty of time for free, independent play. The Nemours Foundation, a large pediatric health system, suggests that kids need at least an hour a day of unstructured playtime.[9] Time spent in front of TV and computer screens doesn't count as independent and free. There are critical developmentally important ways that preschoolers should fill that time by exercising creativity, imagination, and problem-solving skills. Let's take a closer look.

Self-Directed Play

Since kids are often heavily booked with adult-directed activities (or entertained by electronic devices and TV), many have trouble imagining how to occupy themselves on their own. So it's not uncommon to hear, "Mommy! Daddy! Help me. I have nothing to do."

It's productive for kids to be bored and to figure out for themselves how to solve that problem. But, for a parent, it can be hard to ignore such cries of distress. Many of us drop everything and rush to entertain kids, especially when we're trying to get them to consider alternatives to screen time. Or else we list all the possibilities that spring to mind: "Do you want to draw? Do you want to play outside? Do you want to read a book?"

If a child asks, "What should I draw?" we chime in with, "How about a house? A heart? A flower? A sun?"

By filling in the blanks this way, first of all, we're giving our kids ammunition. They're likely to shoot down all the prospects we suggest, if only to make the case for resorting to the Xbox or Wii. But, more importantly, children are exercising power by vetoing rather than by making independent decisions and taking charge of their own fun. Play isn't self-directed if we tell them what to do.

So it's preferable to turn the choice back to the child. You can say, "Okay, we don't have toys handy, but we have a pen and paper. What can we do with them?" Leave it to the child to come up with ideas like Hangman or Tic-Tac-Toe.

Or you can say, "Look around this room. What are the possibilities? What are you in the mood for?"

Or, when the child is drawing, stick to broad strokes of ideas: "Why don't you draw something that you saw today?" Or, "Think of five things you can draw. Then pick one." By inspiring and guiding rather than instructing, you plant the seeds of decision making and help the child to access her creativity.

Imaginative Play

The preschool/kindergarten years are prime time for the blossoming of fantasy. During your child's free play, you may find your home occupied by pirates, fairies, monsters, ghosts, witches, doctors, mommies, daddies, teachers, and so on. Your child may start talking about make-believe friends or animals. These phantom friends do not reflect loneliness but are simply a creative way for your child to try out different relationship scenarios. When your child is three, the line between fantasy and reality may be a little fuzzy, but the distinction should become clearer as she approaches four.

Play Reset

"Play with me!" It's hard to resist that plaintive cry, and there's no question that it's vitally important for us interact with our children. But it's equally critical for them to learn how to entertain themselves. Independent play is the foundation of imagination and much more.

But how can you spark independent play, especially in a child who's come to count on passive, screen-based entertainment or parental attention on demand? Try getting time on your side. Just like a writer staring at a blank page, willing words to come, a child facing an expanse of unstructured time can feel at a loss to fill it. Placing a concrete limit on that time can help:

- **Set a Timer.** Show your child a kitchen timer and set it for ten or fifteen minutes. Say, "When this goes off, we have an appointment. Then we can play together. Until then, you can find something fun to do on your own."

- **Send Your Child Off to Play.** Send the child off to amuse himself while you read a book, make a call, put dinner in the oven, or whatever. Obviously, it's best not to play solitaire on the computer or turn on the TV—activities not permitted for the child during that time.

- **Don't Renegotiate Time.** Resist your child's efforts to renegotiate the time with cries of "But I'm bored." Assure him that the time is short and that you know he'll find something to do. If nothing else, he can get set up for the game that you two will play later.

- **Let Your Child Take the Lead.** When the timer goes off, you're at your child's disposal, but don't spring into tour director mode. Let him decide (within reason) what you're going to do and let him direct the play. The goal is to transfer responsibility for his own entertainment to the child, whether he's playing alone or playing with you. As he becomes more comfortable with the concept, he'll initiate play on his own.

Imaginative play is a natural stage that should be nurtured. Wait to be invited to join in the play. It's fine to suggest ideas, ideally by asking questions like "How would they get to the castle?" But, even if asked, resist trying to dictate the storyline. The whole point, developmentally, is that imaginative play allows your child to develop and control these scenarios, learning to think independently.

Social Play

Around the age of three, a big shift occurs in the way children play together. Younger kids often tend to play side by side, but at preschool age, they start to interact more directly. So it's vitally important for children to have free, unstructured playtime with others their own age.

In the past, neighborhood children would gather in someone's backyard and then tear around the neighborhood all day, with little adult oversight. Today, that wouldn't happen with children of preschool or kindergarten age. Parents expect—and require other parents—to be more involved. But it's possible, and it's important, to supervise adequately without helicoptering.

The imaginative skills kids develop at this age often inspire elaborate fantasy games in which they take on roles that let them explore social relationships. Think of all the capacities these games help instill: sharing, taking turns, cooperating, communicating nonverbally through expressions and actions, leading and following, and resolving conflicts, just to name a few.

When possible, it's best to let children try to negotiate these situations independently. Obviously, you must intervene if a child grows frustrated and gets physical with another—and a certain degree of aggression is fairly typical of preschoolers and kindergartners. But for problems like squabbling over the same toy, you can remind them about taking turns and give them the chance to decide who goes first. They can always draw straws or try to come with some other solution to decide. Empowering kids by encouraging them to create solutions is preferable to hovering and stage managing all their games.

You might be surprised at what they come up with. Children can be endlessly inventive when their creativity is free to blossom.

Child's Play Recap

Here are some age-appropriate guidelines for encouraging children's independent imaginative play.

- **Newborn to Infancy.** Mobiles overhead or an image in a mirror will captivate an infant.

- **Three to Twelve Months.** Play is the main way that a baby begins to engage with the world. She delights in toys that stimulate the senses or that invite manipulation. She loves to grab for an object or scooch toward a parent on the floor. Independent play helps her learn to reason and to understand how her body works. Listening to an adult's soothing voice will also encourage her to experiment with sounds and language.

- **One to Three Years.** Emphasize physical action games and art projects to help your child master motor skills. Encourage fantasy play to help her practice social interactions and foster friendships with other children.

Minimize exposure to digital media before age two. Although free imaginative play offers much greater developmental value, around age two, children can grasp educational TV and computer programs. Watch TV or the computer with your child, and discuss the content with her.

- **Three to Six Years.** Resist weighing down your child with "enrichment" activities. Balance these activities with plenty of unstructured play time.

CHAPTER 6

The Corrections: Self-Discipline and Parental Discipline

"Frannie is becoming very difficult," Gina, her mother, told me. "It's like she started growing defiant when she turned two. The other day, when we were at the playground, she kept throwing sand at other kids. I tried everything. I told her firmly, 'Sand is not for throwing.' That stopped her at first. I distracted her by helping her shovel sand into her bucket. I told her that I'd take her out of the sandbox if she kept it up."

"Did she stop?" I asked. "Did you take her out of the sandbox?"

"No, she kept it up. Maybe I should have removed her, but she loves the sandbox and she did play with the shovel for a while. I thought she was listening until she started throwing sand again. Other parents were getting annoyed, moving their kids away from her, so finally I decided to leave. Frannie pitched a fit, fighting like mad and howling, 'No!' I had to wrestle her into the stroller and strap her in. All the way home, she kept screaming."

Today we often hear that kids are out of control—undisciplined, overindulged, and catered to by parents who have a difficult time standing up to them. Part of the appeal of books like Amy Chua's *Battle Hymn of the Tiger Mother* and Pamela Druckerman's *Bringing Up Bébé*, among others, is the image they evoke of parents firmly in charge—a sharp contrast to the coddling of overindulgent parents. Some look back to the supposedly idyllic past, when children were "seen and not heard," and even suggest that the spankings they endured as children should make a comeback.

In some circles, spanking is advocated not only at home but in schools as well. As of 2012, physical punishment remained legal in schools in nineteen of our fifty states, mostly in the South.[1] This statistic is stunning because in 2006 the United Nations' Committee on the Rights of the Child issued a policy statement recommending that spanking be prohibited; more than thirty countries in the world now ban it, even in the home.[2] Research has consistently shown that physical punishment promotes aggression in children.[3] Furthermore, even if it seems to curb an impulse in a given moment—and it often won't—spanking doesn't work at all as a strategy to change behavior.

To teach your child to control himself, you have to instill in him the desire to want to behave. The first step toward doing so is establishing limits for the child. Children perform much better when they know what is consistently expected of them.

A Line in the Sand: Setting Limits

I think that every parent can identify with Gina's situation. A toddler can often get a fixed idea in her head, like throwing sand. She throws a tantrum when you stop her. Testing limits is natural for toddlers and so is throwing tantrums. From about eighteen months until three years old, children can sometimes try the problem-solving skills of any parent.

It's a lot easier to second-guess another parent's response than it is to curtail misbehavior in the moment. But I had some suggestions to offer that could help Gina cope with Frannie's "terrible twos." I shared with her a playground experience I had when my daughter was two and half, just a little older than Frannie.

> I was alone with both of my children. My son was fussing, and my daughter was determined to go on the swing. "This isn't a good time," I told her. "Your brother is hungry, and I have to feed him. Let's try something that you can do on your own for a while."
>
> "No," she insisted. "Swing!"
>
> "I can't push you on the swing right now. Look around and pick out another place to play."
>
> That didn't dissuade her. She grabbed at the swing and tried to climb up.
>
> "Okay," I said. "You can go on the swing if you want, but remember that I can't push you."
>
> I helped her onto the swing and gave her one push. Then I sat on a bench and started to nurse my son.
>
> It wasn't long before the swing slowed down, and my daughter started calling, "Mommy, Mommy!"

Of course, I was painfully torn. My emotional side wanted to make my daughter happy, even if it meant standing up, bracing my nursing son with one arm, and pushing her with my free hand. But my reasoning side reminded me that I had to keep my word—that two and half was an age when it really mattered to establish ground rules.

So I said, "I'm sorry, but I'm feeding your brother right now. When I'm done, I'll be able to push you."

My daughter was outraged. She threw a tantrum, sitting on that swing, that must have lasted twenty minutes. But giving in would have taught her that she'd get her way if she just screamed long and loud enough. I had to steel myself to sit there calmly and nurse, refusing to respond to her fury.

As I did, other parents who'd witnessed the scenario cheered me on. That was fascinating. "Hang tough," they said. "You're doing the right thing. Stick to your guns."

Rough as the experience was, my daughter did get the message. I stayed consistent, so it took only a few such stand-offs before she accepted that I really meant what I said.

There was a moral to the story, I told Gina. When my daughter insisted on swinging, I agreed, on the condition that I couldn't push her. Once I said that, I couldn't back down if I wanted her to understand. She didn't like waiting to be pushed on the swing, but she chose that option, rejecting other possibilities. The choices we make have consequences, and I couldn't let her think that there would be always be "wiggle room" for her to get exactly what she wanted.

When Gina said that she'd take Frannie out of the sandbox but didn't do it, she set up a situation with wiggle room. Once

Frannie saw that she could stay in the sandbox, no matter what, she was emboldened to keep testing limits. And why not? There was no immediate consequence for throwing sand.

We all hear parents make threats all the time—"If you do X, Y will happen . . ."—but then they don't follow through. Soon grasping that those threats are empty, children keep up the undesirable behavior until the parents are driven to last-ditch measures, like exploding in frustration, or like Gina, leaving the playground angrily. While leaving was certainly appropriate, taking an intermediate step, removing Frannie from the sandbox, would have offered a more powerful lesson—that Gina meant business. That was the message that I felt I had to give my daughter, clearly and unequivocally. I had to set limits.

When do you start setting limits? In a sense, you're setting limits when you sleep-train your child and set up her feeding schedule. But this doesn't become "discipline" per se until the child is old enough to grasp the concept of no. By eight to ten months, when she starts crawling, redirecting her and offering her alternatives to investigate (a plastic container instead of the dog bowl) or safe places to explore will be more effective than constantly chanting, "No, no, no!" By the time a child is around twelve to eighteen months old, she may begin to understand the word *no*, but it will take a few months before she can curtail her actions in response.

Around eighteen months old, many kids will understand when they're doing something forbidden. Antics like throwing food at this age are not acts of defiance so much as experiments, prompted by the wish to see what will happen. Of course, if parents spring to attention and make a fuss, they'll reinforce the throwing behavior. As we discussed in chapter 3, calmly taking the food away for a minute or two can do the trick. At a year to eighteen months, a child may be a little too young to concretely grasp the notion of consequences. But she will begin to understand limits. Repetition—and, above all, consistency—will get the point across.

The Age of Unreason

It's not until your child approaches two that he'll start to connect the dots between his behavior and undesirable results. In other words, he'll begin to grasp that actions have consequences.

That message is most strongly reinforced when the consequences clearly spring from the cause. In the sandbox incident, Gina had a great chance to demonstrate cause and effect to Frannie. As I explained,

> "Taking her out of the sandbox right away would have set up a clear, direct consequence for throwing sand. When she hollered, you'd explain that playing in the sandbox meant 'No throwing.' After giving her a few minutes to calm down, you'd put her back in the sandbox to try again."
>
> "Why put her back?" Gina asked. "Why not take her over to the slide or something?"
>
> "That would have obscured the message," I said. "She'd start playing on the slide and forget the lesson you were trying to teach her. A do-over would give her the chance to show you what she'd learned. And if she threw

sand again, you'd remove her again. She'd get the picture pretty quickly. A repeatable consequence really drives the message home."

Small, repeatable consequences are usually more powerful than bigger gestures, like leaving the playground, which the child may not link as clearly to her specific behavior. The closer the connection between the behavior and the consequence, the more likely the child will be to decide—and even *want*—to do the right thing, to avoid an undesired outcome. After a removal or two, Frannie probably would have chosen independently to stop throwing sand, just to stay in the sandbox—and earned Gina's praise. By tying the consequence directly to the action, Gina would have made the point that throwing sand was not acceptable. She would have kept her word rather than make a meaningless threat. Staying calm also sends the critical message to your child that you are in control and that she isn't going to get a reaction out of you with her misbehavior.

And—importantly—by giving Frannie another chance in the sandbox, Gina would have demonstrated her trust. Trust in the child's willingness and ability to change is a critical component of discipline. Trust motivates children, just as it does adults. We're all much more inclined to try to live up to the expectations of someone who has faith in us.

What if Frannie didn't stop throwing sand? Then Gina could continue to remove her from the sandbox every few minutes, to show her that the same behavior would have the same consequence every time.

Empowering children to seek alternatives is also important. Say that your child wants to go on the swings, and another child beats him to the last unoccupied one. He has a fit. You certainly don't want to fight the other mother for that swing. Giving in to a child who's tantruming will only reinforce the behavior. At times, we all lose out on things, even undeservedly. Your child may respond favorably if you say, "We'll come back. Isn't there something else we could do? Let's look around and see what else looks fun and free. I'll race you there!"

When dealing with a tantruming child, it can help to get down on his level, to look him in the eye and really get his attention. Sometimes it's better not to talk at all but simply to stand nearby or to comfort him. This is especially true if you can't keep the annoyance or anxiety out of your voice. Sensing your tension will only stoke his agitation.

Of course, there will be plenty of times when these intermediate steps are not effective. Say that you're grocery shopping and your toddler throws a tantrum. Try some of the steps listed in the Stormy Weather sidebar on page 140. If they don't work, abandon your shopping cart and leave the store with your child.

Meltdown Remediation

Hard as they are to endure, it's normal for kids to throw tantrums. Toddlers are making huge developmental strides—walking, interacting, imagining, and much more—but haven't yet learned to process all of the intense emotions that flood them. They also don't yet have the language skills to express them. No wonder they blow up! How can parents help children outgrow the tantrum stage?

The first line is setting limits, refusing to respond to a child's demands when they're made in a tantrum state. You can say, "I can't hear you when you're so upset. I want to listen if you'll use your words calmly to tell me what you are feeling." Setting

Stormy Weather

The time when toddlers are most volatile is often called the "terrible twos," but that's a misnomer. This stage emerges at different times in different kids. For many, it begins between twelve and eighteen months, while for some the year between the ages of three and four is stormier than the "twos."

Can meltdowns be prevented? No, but it's possible to head off some of them and cope with the others in a way that can lessen their force. Here are some strategies you can use to try to head them off:

- **Know your child's limitations.** Don't drag her to a restaurant brunch that coincides with naptime or expect her to join you on errands when she's hungry. That's just too much to ask.

- **Give her activities to stave off boredom,** like a new coloring book to use at a restaurant. When I took my young children to the supermarket, I offered them the chance to help pick out food, as discussed in chapter 3, which had the other benefit of making them more likely to eat it. I also let them choose one special treat now and then, an item that I might not otherwise buy. Be careful with such incentives, though. You don't want them to learn to expect bribes for not throwing a tantrum. Think empowerment, not payoff.

that limit gives the child a choice—to articulate his desires if he wants them to be met.

But to teach toddlers and preschoolers, especially, to organize their thoughts, I encourage parents to talk through their own

---

When the storm clouds do gather, weather tantrums well:

- **Stay calm.** Shouting or scolding will only escalate the tantrum.

- **Make sure that your child is in a safe environment** where she can't hurt herself if she, say, kicks something or where she's not surrounded by breakable objects.

- **Change the location.** Sometimes, simply taking your child outdoors will divert her enough to quell the outburst. If you're out somewhere, sitting in the car (with you) for a short time may help.

- **If your child is in a public place** where's she's disturbing others, like a restaurant or a store, **be prepared to leave.** Don't beg or keep threatening or warning. If there's a lull in the storm, give her one chance by saying, "This is not how we act in restaurants. If you can sit down now, we'll stay. If you can't, we're going home." If that doesn't work, be sure to leave.

- **Don't scold or punish your child for having tantrums.** Let them blow over. Later, if it seems appropriate, you can discuss what got her so upset.

- **Be consistent and patient.** The more consistent you are in your approach to tantrums, the sooner your child will learn to master her emotions. But, by sooner, I don't mean days. It may take weeks or months before your kid is developmentally able to process disappointment more rationally. But it *will* happen!

---

problem-solving process aloud. Hearing how you handle disappointing situations gives kids a vocabulary—an emotional, cognitive, and verbal blueprint—for coping with emotions. It's good to keep the reflection simple. An example might go like this:

> "Brian, remember the night I wanted Chinese food for dinner and Daddy wanted pizza?"
>
> "Yes, I do! You didn't get what you wanted. We ordered pizza," Brian recalled.
>
> "But Brian, I ordered pizza with mushrooms and broccoli so I had the same vegetables I would have ordered if we had Chinese food. It was a compromise and then the next time I got to choose what we had."

I do these "talk throughs" with my own kids all the time. Breaking down your thoughts shows children, concretely, how to analyze a problem. It literally gives them a script to help counter overwhelming frustration. And it shows them that they're not alone in being thwarted—that even adults don't always get what they want.

The Penalty Box

It's very common for children to test the limits with their parents to see where the boundaries lie. Sometimes they express themselves physically and other times verbally.

> "Bobby's getting so bratty," Lynn complained. "We just got through the 'terrible twos,' so I thought we were due for a breather. But now that he's three and a half, he's getting really fresh. The other day he refused to do something I asked and told me to shut up."

"What did you do?" I asked.

"Well, I tried not to overreact. I did scold him, saying, 'You don't tell Mommy to shut up.' But he just sort of laughed and ran away. I got so mad that I didn't even chase after him. I needed to calm down.

"Later, Bobby acted like nothing happened, but I was still upset. My husband thinks the mouthing off is no big deal. But these days, Bobby is disrespectful all the time. I really don't like it."

Lynn was aware that she and her husband had to reach an agreement about Bobby's new behavior. For a correction to take hold, a child's parents and caretakers all have to hold the same line. But I assured her that Bobby's mouthing off was not unusual. Children are sponges. They constantly pick up new words and attitudes, and, of course, they want to test them out. What better way to see how they'll fly than to bounce them off their parents?

Lynn was right not to overreact in the moment, which would just make using the inappropriate language more appealing to Bobby. As for "acting like nothing happened," for Bobby, nothing much did. He was just butting heads with his mother in a typical preschool bout of testing limits. But since he was acting disrespectful, it was time for parental intervention.

"Do you give him time-outs?" I asked.

"We tried that when he was younger," Lynn said. "But they didn't really work. It was always a big fight to get him to sit there and stay put. We wound up giving him more attention during time-outs than if we scolded him. But scolding doesn't seem to be working anymore."

Some children don't grasp time-outs when they're younger, but for preschoolers, they can be very effective. So I encouraged Lynn to give time-outs another try.

We talked over the basic process. Time-outs are most successful when a parent can impose them firmly, rather than angrily, and without engaging the child in an argument.

1. **Explain ahead of time what behavior will result in a time-out.** Explain to your child ahead of time that specific behaviors, like yelling at Mommy when asked to do something or using bad words and expressions like "shut up," will lead to a time-out. Warn that resisting a time-out will have consequences.

2. **Decide where the time-out will take place.** The location should be somewhere that it's safe to leave the child unsupervised and that is boring but not scary. Some parents stick the child in a chair in the corner of the room, facing the wall, but I prefer sending them to another room, away from the main activity of the house. That way, they can't chime in on conversations when they're supposed to be isolated.

3. **Give a single warning.** When time-out-worthy behavior is brewing, give the child a single warning, just to let her know why she'll be getting the time-out. Don't keep threatening, or you'll defeat your purpose. If one warning doesn't check the behavior, impose the time-out immediately. Don't wait or scold, don't discuss. Just do it.

4. **Set a timer.** Set a timer at the outset of the time-out, so the child will have a concrete sense of the minutes passing. The rule of thumb for time-outs is one minute for year of life.

A child who's very angry may need an extra minute or so to get to the designated time-out spot, so wait until she's in position before you start the clock. Warn her that asking when she can come out will add a minute to her time.

5. **Resist efforts to escape from the time-out.** Yes, she can go to the bathroom, but let her know that you'll tack the minutes she takes on to the end of her time.

6. **Discuss the behavior when calm.** If you want to discuss the behavior that prompted the time-out, don't do it while you or the child is still upset.

7. **Be consistent.** Apply time-outs for specific behaviors rather than randomly, and use them every time those behaviors occur.

8. **Don't expect instant results.** It can take a number of time-outs before your child starts to curb the behavior.

By following these guidelines, you should find that time-outs will start to make a difference.

The Master Plan

Time-outs are very useful for certain kinds of behavior, like frank disobedience. When a child throws a ball in the house more than once, taking it away is a direct and appropriate consequence. However, when there's no ball to take away, a time-out can be the equivalent. But to keep it an effective technique, you don't want to overuse it.

So, for smaller infractions, like being mean to a sibling, I recommend having the child make a more comprehensive chart with a ladder drawn on it, like the one described on page 103 for toilet training. Let's call this the "master chart."

The master chart is used to record both positive and negative behavior. You can have columns for different categories that you and the child decide need work, such as getting along with a sibling, doing chores, and obeying. The middle rung of the chart is the starting point, and the child has a Velcro sticker to use in each column. For each "good" deed, like putting away

Corrections Reset

Consistency is the foundation of discipline, but in some instances, you may not have been as vigilant as you might have wished. Say, for example, that you've wound up with a preschooler or kindergartner who swats his younger brother. (I'm not talking about violence here, but basic older-kid frustration.) You can and should discuss the reasons for his frustration, but you also have to lay down the law, concretely demonstrating that hitting is not acceptable. To do so, you have to establish a clear penalty for the behavior. It can make a big difference if you enlist your child in deciding what that penalty will be. Together, choose a penalty that is

- **Repeatable and particular to the behavior,** so the child will associate the behavior with the penalty.

- **Reasonable—of the same magnitude as the misbehavior— but still undesirable.** Never withhold something a child really needs, like a meal, as a penalty.

- **Scheduled to be exacted shortly, if not immediately,** after the behavior occurs.

An example of an ineffective penalty for hitting is, say, forbidding the child to visit Grandma on the coming weekend. First of all, toys at the end of the day, the sticker in each column moves up a rung; for each instance of disobeying by, say, using a bad word, the sticker moves down a rung. When a sticker reaches the top of its column, the child gets a reward that he's chosen, like a night at the movies. When a sticker reaches the bottom of its column, there is a consequence, also chosen by the child, like lost playdates (see the Corrections Reset sidebar below for tips on choosing penalties for misbehavior).

it's not repeatable. If you exacted that penalty for one instance of hitting, you'd have to impose a new one if he hit his brother again. So he would never come to associate a specific deterrent with hitting.

Second, the penalty is out of proportion to the error. One smack should not cost the child a whole afternoon with Grandma.

Finally, the penalty is too far in the future. By the time the weekend rolls around, the child won't connect the penalty to the "crime."

A more effective penalty would be giving up a period of TV viewing or computer use for each hitting incident. The goal is that eventually—and it may take some repetition—whenever he raises a hand to his brother, he'll think, "Wait, there goes my TV time."

If he's helped to set the penalty himself, he'll internalize that message even more indelibly. For example, ahead of time you can ask your child what you think the right consequence for hitting his brother should be. Perhaps he'll suggest having to go to his room for four minutes. The next time he hits his brother, remind him the he decided the punishment would be four minutes in his room. You didn't impose the consequence—he chose it. If he hits his brother anyway, knowing what would happen, he can only blame herself. That's a powerful feedback loop, one more likely than parental intervention to motivate him to change his behavior.

The sample master chart below shows how the ladder can be set up, using examples of behavior to work on, rewards, and consequences, with stickers to move up and down the rungs. (In my house, we use Velcro for the stickers because it's easier to move them up and down.)

The beauty of the master chart is that it helps children embrace responsibility for their actions, because they can track

Master Chart

Setting the Table	Cleaning Up Room	Talking Nicely
Reward *Movie Night*	Reward *Trip to the Mall*	Reward *Pottery Date*
+5	+5	+5
+4	+4	+4
+3	+3	+3
+2	+2	+2
+1	+1	+1
Start	Start	Start
-1	-1	-1
-2	-2	-2
-3	-3	-3
-4	-4	-4
-5	-5	-5
Consequence *No Playdates for 2 Days*	Consequence *No TV for a Night*	Consequence *No Computer for 2 days*

them just as they'd mark their progress when playing a game. Proud of the columns in which the stickers are moving up, kids get very motivated to keep doing good deeds to push them to the top and "win." When stickers are nearing the bottom of columns, kids really make an effort to check their behavior to avoid earning consequences and "losing."

It's much more satisfying—almost fun—to think of their behavior as progressive steps than as the genesis of a litany of half-remembered scoldings. The chart is empowering because it shows kids, graphically, that an independent choice underlies each action they make. Whether they ultimately "win" or lose" is entirely in their hands.

There's another benefit of the master chart, but this one is for parents. Because the chart also highlights positive actions, it reminds us that the flip side of correction is encouragement and praise. It's all too easy, when dealing with kids, to grow deaf to our own monotone of disapproving words like *No, Stop it, Don't, Watch it, Wait. . . .*

We don't want to drown our kids in empty praise, but the positive actions they mark on the chart can prompt us not just to correct them but to keep helping them set new goals.

My daughter, at age nine, once said something incredibly wise: that self-discipline is doing something not because you're asked, but because you know that it's what you want to do.

It's a thought that I often reflect on when patients' parents ask me about discipline. The essence of effective discipline is not punishing kids but instilling in them the desire to do the right thing—to prompt them to decide, independently, to change their behavior.

The Corrections Recap

Here are at-a-glance discipline tips for kids of various ages, aimed at helping them develop the independent capacity for self-control. Spanking is not only an ineffective mode of discipline, but it also teaches the bad lesson that it is appropriate to retaliate physically.

- **Eight to Eighteen Months.** Redirecting and offering safe alternative activities will usually be more effective at altering behavior than scolding, "No, no, no."

- **Eighteen Months.** Setting limits—establishing a consistent consequence for every instance of undesired behavior (for example, taking away the plate every time a child throws food)—will be the most effective way to get the point across.

- **Twenty-Four Months.** Help your child understand that actions have consequences: be sure that the consequence immediately follows the action, is clearly tied to the action, and is consistently applied. Small, repeatable consequences are easier to grasp than grand (but confusing) gestures. Even more confusing are empty threats. The repeatable consequences strategy affords the child a "do-over." Providing a do-over demonstrates trust in the child and faith in her ability to change.

- **Twelve Months to Four Years.** The tantrums of the terrible twos (at any time from twelve months to four years) are natural meltdowns by a child without the vocabulary or the familiarity with emotions to cope with intense feelings. Stay calm, make sure that the child is in a safe place and can't hurt herself or do damage, and let the storms blow over. Later, discuss what got the child distressed. Know your child's limitations and provide distractions to ease her frustration. Giving in to a child's demands during a tantrum will only reinforce the behavior.

- **Three to Six Years.** Unacceptable behavior requires a firm parental response. Time-outs can be a very effective deterrent and are most successful if parents impose them without anger or argument. Warn the child, in advance, that certain behavior will result in a time-out and that resisting a time-out will also have consequences. Time-outs should be repeatable, clearly linked to and of the same magnitude as the infraction, and implemented immediately following the infraction. They should be reserved for serious misbehavior.

  For minor slipups, have the child mark "good" and "bad" actions on a chart—good actions lead to a reward and bad actions lead to punishment. Motivation is stronger if your child chooses her own rewards and punishments.

CHAPTER 7

The Daily Drill: Tasks and Responsibilities

A new patient's father introduced himself as Bill, adding, "And this is Charlotte."

"Hi, Charlotte," I said. I saw from her chart that she was almost four. "What a pretty skirt."

She had on a ruffled pink skirt over green-and-black striped leggings, topped by a sequined orange T-shirt. Glittery flip-flops adorned her feet.

"Charlotte loves colors," Bill said a little sheepishly.

"I put this on too," Charlotte said, plucking at her T-shirt with pride.

"All by yourself? That's wonderful!" I said, and I meant it. "It's great when kids dress creatively and independently," I told Bill.

It delights me to see children come to my office in outfits like Charlotte's—not only because of the individuality they express but also because they reflect such initiative. From toddler age on, kids are capable of performing so many more daily tasks, such as dressing, than a lot of parents recognize. What's more, children often want—and, developmentally speaking, need—to handle them independently. They are wired to become self-reliant.

Of course, a kid working alone or even with supervision inevitably takes far longer to accomplish the same goal than an adult. Children's motor skills are still evolving throughout the preschool and kindergarten years, as are their powers of concentration. So they dawdle, losing focus on the task at hand. They succumb to every distraction. Modern parents acclimated to an on-demand world find it challenging to cope with child time.

Children's efforts can have an unpredictable outcome, as Charlotte's vibrant outfit shows. Still, assuming responsibility for the daily drill—the normal activities of life—is such an important rite of passage that parents should actively promote it, even at the expense of time. If you redo a child's every effort, you're not teaching responsibility or showing him you have confidence in his ability.

It's About Time

In the interests of raising awareness, let's look at some of the ways that even conscientious parents tend to discourage children's assumption of responsibility. Most of us tend to intervene more than is, strictly speaking, necessary, often for the sake of saving time—at the expense of our children's self-reliance.

Locomotion

In the introduction, I mentioned what I call sherpa parents, always staggering under the backbreaking burden of myriad bags and clinging children. We all love to pick up our kids and carry them, but once children are mobile, it pays to make sherpa duty the exception rather than the default procedure. Once kids realize that it's quicker and easier to be carried or wheeled in a stroller—and when they sense your exasperation at their slow pace—they start to resist walking on their own. When you consider that, between the ages of two and five, most kids are still developing balance and coordination, as well as learning to focus their attention, you can see why it's so important not to just scoop them up and lug them from point A to point B.

Active, independent play helps kids hone their motor skills, but just walking from the house to the car or from the bus stop to the store is also critical. Let's face it—in our car-centered culture, most adults don't get in the amount of walking each day that will benefit their health. For children, walking is not just a matter of exercise; it's important for physical development, too.

Yes, kids are poky. Adults walking with them have to slow to a crawl and echo their stops and starts. When you have to, you can speed kids up by giving them a focus. You can race your child to a certain point or say, "I'll carry you as far as the yellow sign, and then from there you can walk."

But doesn't it behoove us all, in our high-speed culture, to resist the constant pressure to rush around? Does getting somewhere a couple minutes sooner really make that big a difference? Giving kids the message that they're competent and, most of the time, able to function on their own steam is far more likely to be life-changing.

The same kind of patience should apply to processes like easy climbs. I often see parents lifting fully capable children into the car, rather than letting them climb in themselves. In my office, I have a stepstool to help children get on and off the examination table. Lots of parents bypass it, lifting kids who are clearly able to get up on their own. They're likely the same parents who always hang up their kids' jackets for them or get them undressed and dressed. They may not see their actions as helicoptering, but the effect undermines self-reliance. A child who's struggling a little with a task needs practice more than rescue.

And what about all those bags sherpas schlep? Even children as young as three enjoy having their own little wheeled backpacks to pull. Of course, they won't keep track of them perfectly, but encouraging kids to manage them plants the seeds of responsibility. It also gives them a tremendous sense of pride.

Communication

Learning to speak is a critical communication and social skill. Parents can nearly always read their children's points, grunts, and other nonverbal expressions, and grow to more or less anticipate their kids' needs. So when words start to emerge from the child's babble, around twelve to eighteen months of age, parents may not feel a burning need to foster speech. After all, they can understand the child. But it's important for other people to be able to understand his words, so I often advise parents to resist the urge to "fill in the blanks."

Independent communication is such a powerful tool that it should be actively nurtured. Even before the child starts forming actual words, there is a lot you can do to foster social communication. When you look at pictures together, he'll delight in responding to give-and-takes like "What does the horse say?" "Neigh!" "What does the cow say?" "Moo!" It can be very helpful, when your child is twelve to twenty-four months old, to teach him the words for parts of his body, like "toes," and things in his environment, like "couch," "chair," and "dish," enunciating clearly to help him grasp them. A child whose vocabulary is building slowly may benefit if you engage his interests, as Maureen, his mother, started to do when my patient Brendan was about eighteen months old.

> "Brendan is so crazy about cars," she said. "We have little ones that were always his favorite toys. He would go, 'vroom,' when he pushed them. When we were driving, he'd point out the window at vehicles, making motor-like sounds and laughing. So we started teaching him the names of distinctive ones, like 'truck.' He was calling everything 'duck' until we began to show him that there were different cars like 'Honda' and 'SUV.' Within a couple months, he could actually tell cars apart and name them. The other day, he said 'BNW' when we saw a BMW and also spotted a 'Toy-ta-ta.' It's so funny! Those are the words he loves to say the most."

When your child starts to use words, don't rush to correct his mistakes. Give him time to try to articulate them and then correct his pronunciation in an encouraging way, like saying, "That's right! It's a *truck*." Your welcoming tone and affirmation will invite him to experiment with speech.

By around age two, most kids will amass a vocabulary of at least fifty words and start to form little sentences, progressing to enjoying more sophisticated constructs by age three.

It's important for parents of kids from two years old on, and extending into preschool, to hold back and let children form their own thoughts and speak independently. Don't finish their sentences for them, even if they seem to be struggling. Don't answer when they're asked questions. Don't embellish what they say with details that they can't yet articulate.

When we hear kids straining for words, these interventions spring to our tongues almost automatically. But if we step in and speak for our children, we're telling them that, in effect, they needn't bother to take on the challenge of expressing themselves. Why should they? When we supply answers, we're telling kids that they don't have to engage with questioners—and depriving them of the pleasure of interacting. When they do manage to answer but we elaborate, we diminish the interaction they've accomplished by implying that their words aren't good enough.

Of course, I'm not saying that you should never answer or fill in details when, say, the doctor asks how your child is feeling or in other situations when the whole story matters. But most of the time, it's better to suppress the reflex that makes us want to fill in the blanks and get the conversation moving. Waiting for the child to craft a response is time well spent; it's like a vote of confidence, showing that he's doing well speaking independently, without your micromanagement. It shows that he can rely on his own power of speech. If there is more to a story, you can engage him in conversation and ask questions, but let him remain in charge of the conversation.

Even when your child grows comfortable with language, keep in mind that it will still be a challenge for him to process his thoughts. If you ask a preschooler a general question, such as, "How's your class going?" you'll probably get a one-word answer, like "Fine." He'll likely find it too daunting to sort out his impressions and come up with a meaningful reply.

But if you ask a more specific question, such as, "Who did you play with in school today?" you're apt to spark a potential conversation: "I played with Johnny on the slide at the playground. He fell down, and he cried. Ms. Burns put a Band-Aid on his finger, and he felt better. . . ."

In my family, we've adopted a ritual that I have heard the Obama family, among others, uses to stimulate dinner conversation. It's a game called Roses and Thorns. We go around the table, and each person describes one good thing (a rose) and one bad thing (a thorn) that happened that day. It's a great chance for parents to model for kids how they cope with everyday conflicts and also to highlight the fact that life is full of small pleasures.

In these discussions, parents give kids unconscious scripts for expressing ideas and for telling simple stories. For example, even a mundane report like the following has a storyline, with a beginning (what happened), a middle (why it was interesting), and a conclusion: *Today I had lunch with my friend, and I tried something I never had before. It was a dessert from India, which was like cottage cheese in honey syrup. It was really delicious . . .*

When children share their roses and thorns, parents can celebrate their triumphs and guide them through disappointments. The game, importantly, also lets kids practice generating conversation independently, without waiting to be "drawn out." And parents might learn things that might otherwise fly under the radar, like the time my son confessed, "Today my thorn was fighting and getting sent to the principal's office."

Ouch! Oh well, what a perfect launch for a discussion of conflict resolution.

To encourage independent sharing, I always advise parents to resist the urge to stage-manage their kids' communications. Saying, "Tell Grandma about that big dog next door . . . " doesn't leave your child the freedom to initiate his own interaction. Let him come up with what he wants to tell Grandma on his own.

We all have times when we don't feel like sharing. When your child is in one of those moods, don't push. Respect his frame of mind but show that you're always available by saying, "I get the sense that you don't feel like talking this morning. Just know that if anything happens—whether it's special or something that makes you sad—I'd love to hear about it, whenever you want to tell me."

Morning Madness

For most families, stress peaks in the morning. There's just so much to do! Everyone has to wake up on time; wash faces and hands; brush teeth; comb hair; get dressed; eat breakfast; clear the dishes; assemble papers, homework, lunches, projects, and anything else that has to be brought to work or school; and somehow leave the house at the appointed hour.

Now is the time you'll feel grateful if you let your two-year-old start dressing herself. At three or four, getting ready for preschool, she'll have it down to a science. If your child hasn't reached that level yet, you can speed the morning routine by having her lay out two possible outfits, along with underwear, shoes, and socks, the night before. Ideally, they'll both be easy to put on, dresses and leggings or elastic-waist pants and pull-over tops. All she'll have to do is choose one and be ready to go. Giving her a choice both forestalls the what-to-wear battle and underscores the fact that picking out clothes and getting dressed is her responsibility.

As your child gets older, she'll very likely develop her own taste and sense of style, as Charlotte did. Of course, there will be times—say, for important events—when you have to tailor her creations to the occasion. But think how much fun it will be for her to get dressed on regular days, when she gets to create her own ensemble.

Of course, before getting dressed, she'll have to wash up and brush her teeth. At eighteen months, many kids want to brush their own teeth, which you should encourage, with the caveat that you may need to finish the job. By the age of two, most children are able to wash their own hands, but they may need some coaching through face washing. But by around age three, a child should be able to brush her own teeth in the morning.

How do you ensure that kids do a good tooth-brushing job? Of course, you'll want to check their teeth afterward. Some dentists suggest that, if a young child does morning brushing, parents give her teeth a more thorough going-over before bed.

What I recommend is that parents train kids well, using one of the many tooth-brushing songs and perhaps a light-up electric toothbrush. The Internet is full of such lyrics, many of them set to the tune of "Row, Row, Row Your Boat." You can sing while your child brushes, following the directions in the lyrics to reach all sections of teeth, then gradually extract yourself from the bathroom as she learns the song and gets the hang of the process.

Electric toothbrushes that light up, with a resetting timer—it will flash after, say, thirty seconds to signal the child to move on to another batch of teeth—can be really helpful. Because it's fun, the light-up function can be very motivating.

In chapter 3, we talked about children as young as three being able to fix their own breakfasts. You can facilitate this process by having your child set the table the night before.

And what about the job of assembling all material that a child needs to take to school? That's not a task you want to personally have to accomplish, along with everything else, in the morning. Again, the night before is the time to stuff the backpacks and put them by the front door. Kids can develop the habit of putting homework in their backpacks as soon as they're done with it. While a three-year-old can't be expected to remember what she's supposed to bring to school, a picture chart can be a helpful tool to pave the way for later on. On the chart she can either draw or cut out images of the items that need to be packed each morning like her folder, a snack, and her lunch bag. By four or five, the child should be able to shoulder some responsibility for packing up, subject to a parental final check.

I've detailed the kinds of responsibilities kids can assume, not to create a false picture of utopian mornings when parents wake at leisure, then shower and dress undisturbed, but to illustrate the many points at which parents can opt out of the daily drill. So many of us think it saves time if we micromanage it all—chasing kids around the house to wash and dress them, sorting through the toy box for show-and-tell prospects, collecting homework for older kids, flipping pancakes with one

continued on page 164

Morning Madness Game Plan

The most effective way to get kids on track in the morning is to set up a clear routine. Children do best with a definite game plan—even a sign posted on the wall—to remind them of each task that has to be performed. Use graphics for children too young to read—a picture of a toothbrush, say. Depending on your child's age, here are some possible morning tasks to list on the sign:

- Use the bathroom.

- Wash face and hands.

- Get dressed.

- Check backpack for necessary school supplies.

- Eat breakfast.

- Wash hands and brush teeth.

- Comb hair.

Sit down with your child and make the sign together, so you can put the tasks in the order she prefers. Maybe she'd rather eat breakfast before getting dressed, for example. Once your child gets the ritual down, the sign may no longer be necessary.

What to do about dawdling? A two-year-old has little grasp of time or the concept of lateness. By three, children are more cognizant of time but will still need prodding. Remember that part of the point of the morning routine is to avoid standing over your children, nagging and cracking the whip. Instead, here are some ways to help dawdlers:

- Expect to need extra time and build it into your schedule.

- If it will help your child, you can set a kitchen timer for, say, the washing and dressing part of the ritual, so she can hear the minutes ticking down. A clock with a face may also help.

Although children can't usually tell time until the age of six or so, they can see the hand moving toward the 3 or the 6 or the 9—whatever interval you've told them they have for a particular step. You can draw a picture of the clock face on the sign, showing the point when that step should be completed.

- Give up to three warnings, announcing the time they have left for a particular step, and then withdraw. Make sure they know the consequence for being late and be consistent. For example, if they are ready for school, they get special story time or they are allowed to listen to music in the car on the way to school. If not, they don't get that privilege. The master chart on page 148 can be a great motivator here.

- Add "Getting Ready" as an expectation on the master chart. For each day that the child is ready to go on time, the sticker moves up a level, and it moves down a level for each instance of avoidable lateness. When the sticker reaches the top of the column, the child gets a reward; if it sinks to the bottom, there's a penalty that's bigger than for a single infraction.

- Set up a race: The first child to get washed and dressed and make it to the breakfast table gets to move her sticker up an extra level. Or make it a challenge to see who can get ready first—child or parents.

Even if the child continues to dawdle, be sure to praise her for what she does manage to accomplish: "You did a great job putting on your clothes. Perhaps tomorrow you will be even faster and have enough time to brush your teeth on time, too!"

Remember that, for a two- or three-year-old, washing your face and getting dressed on your own is no easy feat. Eventually, pride in her achievements may make getting ready less of a daily struggle. She'll say, proudly, "Look, I did it myself."

continued from page 161

hand while slapping together lunches with the other, pulling on our clothes while shouting at dawdlers, nagging everyone to brush their teeth, piling everyone into the car, running back in the house to retrieve forgotten items, and so on. What a prescription for chaos and unnecessary stress!

If we transfer at least some of these responsibilities to our kids, we both empower them and make mornings less hectic for the whole family. The Morning Madness Game Plan sidebar on page 162 offers a game plan for getting mornings to move smoothly.

I Am Responsible

There have been many instances when my children have surprised me with their own initiative and ownership of tasks. The following anecdote illustrates one of these examples.

My son brought home a project from preschool that really touched me. It was a flower that he'd drawn on a sheet of paper. At the center of the flower was the caption I AM RESPONSIBLE.

On each petal of the flower, the teacher had written a task that my son had told her was his responsibility. I was really charmed by some of them, including, "Bring in the newspaper" and "Bring in the garbage cans."

At that age, my son was too small to wrestle two heavy garbage cans out of the garage and out to the curb. But he was able to bring the empty cans in after the trash was collected. As for the newspaper, every morning it was dropped at the top of our driveway, sheathed in plastic. Once or twice I asked him to pick it up. Then he decided, on his own, to assume the daily responsibility of bringing the paper into the house and bringing the cans in while I got the car packed for the day.

I was so proud of him for taking that initiative—and so touched by his obvious satisfaction at doing these "grownup" jobs.

It is important for children to have family responsibilities as they contribute to a sense of self-worth and confidence. Parents are often surprised by how capable their children actually are. There was an article in the *New Yorker* about an anthropologist, Carolina Izquierdo, who studied kids from two radically different populations: a tribe living along the Amazon River in Peru and the upper middle class in Los Angeles. The results of the study were predictable. While the tribal toddlers were able to heat their own food over open fires and cut grass with machetes at the age of three, the coddled LA teenagers could barely work the labor-saving devices in their homes. One reason for the vast difference, the anthropologist noted, was that for many Los Angeles parents, it took "more effort to get children to collaborate than to do the tasks themselves."[1]

This is yet another cautionary tale about helicopter parenting, with a strong warning about the false economy of time we gain by doing everything for our kids. The few minutes or often seconds we think we're saving in given moments can quash initiative and a sense of personal competence in children.

The article also highlights how much toddlers are capable of doing by themselves. Of course, I'm not suggesting that you should let yours anywhere near the stove or send him out to mow the lawn. But from toddlerhood on, children can take on everyday duties in the family and, in fact, need to do so, to develop a sense of responsibility. What's more, helping out around the house can really boost their self-esteem.

> Four-year-old Justin beamed as his mother, Erica, told me about his job. "He's in charge of setting the dinner table," she said. "We have a set of plates that are different colors, so each night he decides which ones to use. Last night we had yellow, and Justin chose green napkins to go with them. He has a terrific sense of color."
>
> "How wonderful," I said to Justin. "It sounds like you enjoy setting the table."
>
> "It's a big help," he declared. "And Mommy can cook."
>
> Erica smiled at me. She'd complained on earlier office visits about Justin's wildness when she got home from work. He ran around like crazy, demanding her full attention, just when she was trying to get dinner on the table. I'd suggested he might settle down if she let him contribute to the effort.
>
> "Yes," Erica said. "It's such a great help. It makes cooking dinner so much easier for me."

Interestingly, children actually seem to be hardwired to be helpful. A number of studies have shown that children as young as eighteen months old will come to the aid of an adult who has dropped something or whose arms are too full to open a cabinet. Kids do so spontaneously, not because they're expecting a reward. Researchers describe this behavior as a kind of natural altruism that parents can build on as their children grow.[2]

This quality doesn't necessarily translate into picking up toys or putting dirty clothes in the hamper. Helping seems to be a critical factor. But it does suggest that asking kids for help can be a powerful incentive. That seemed to be true for Justin, as well as for my son.

Recognizing how critical responsibilities are in building children's self-reliance, how can parents encourage kids to embrace them? The place to start is with clear, realistic expectations. The What's My Job? sidebar on page 168 shows the kinds of tasks that children can readily assume at various ages.

Obviously, some of these capabilities will vary with each child. Some of them should be considered givens rather than chores: once a kid can dress and undress himself, he can put his dirty clothes in the hamper; and one who can take out toys to play with can put them back on the shelf. Singing a tune together, like Barney's "Clean Up" song (many others are available on the Internet), can help to motivate a child.

Beyond these expected tasks, parents may want to assign an extra daily job to a child, like setting the table or feeding the cat—something that's not too difficult, which the child can make his own—and perhaps a weekly one as well. Ideally, these will be age-appropriate duties that your child at least somewhat enjoys and can take pride in handling.

They should also be contributions that hold real value for you. For example, when I was a child, I wasn't expected to make my bed. I started making my bed in college and now do it every morning, but since I rarely did it as a child, I don't require it of my kids. Bed making may be important to you, but because it isn't to me, I wouldn't assign it as a chore. I prefer to have my children do things that, to me, really matter.

As kids grow older, their chores should increase in complexity. I don't think any child should graduate from grade school, say, without knowing how to do the laundry or make a meal. If you start early, by the time college rolls around, they will be masters.

What's My Job?

Age Two. Pick up toys and put them on a shelf or in a toy chest, put dirty clothes in the hamper and throw trash in the wastebasket, help sort laundry into lights and darks.

Age Three. Water plants or feed pets, clean up her own spills, help clear the table, serve herself breakfast or a simple snack, put her clean, folded clothes in dresser drawers.

Age Four. Set the table, take forks and spoons out of the dishwasher, dust, help with simple cooking tasks.

Age Five and Six. Make her bed, empty small wastebaskets, pack her own backpack, help sort recycling items.

Dos and Don'ts for Children's Chores

The What's My Job sidebar above will help you determine what chores are age-appropriate for your children. It is important, though, to keep the following dos and don'ts in mind for children's chores.

- **Do make your expectations for both daily and weekly chores very clear.** Write them down, or for toddlers, use graphics.

- **Do make chores part of an established daily or weekly routine,** to be performed at roughly the same time each day or same day each week. Letting the child approach them haphazardly makes it far less likely that they'll get done, and nagging is rarely an effective tactic with procrastinators.

- **Do keep your child company while he's doing chores,** at least until he gets familiar with them. Just being with you is a major motivator for your kids. But don't rush to help him with his tasks. The point is for the child to do the work.

- **Do create a chores column on the master chart** described on page 148 for your child's assigned tasks.

- **Don't pay your children for doing chores.** An allowance can be used to teach the child to handle money, but tying it to chores implies that they're not a fact of life but something special that deserves compensation. If your child does something beyond the call of duty, like helping you clean out the garage, come up with a fitting reward, like a special outing.

- **Don't expect perfection, and don't redo your children's chores.** If necessary, review the job and show the child how to improve it. Praise your child when he's made an honest effort, even if the results aren't flawless.

- **Don't burden kids with constant chores** that can overwhelm them, or you may have a rebellion on your hands. Remember that, up through the preschool years, free play is your child's main job.

I Am Accountable

Once your child is around five years old, you should introduce the notion of accountability. By that, I mean accepting and living with the consequences of her actions. Imparting this lesson can be hard for parents because it means resisting the natural impulse to bail a child out of difficulties.

Imagine this scenario:

Your child can't decide what to have for breakfast. There's cereal on the table, which she refuses. You offer to make an egg or a toaster waffle. She says no to both.

"Okay," you say, "Check the refrigerator and see what looks good to you."

But nothing in the fridge appeals to her. At that point, you warn her, "The carpool is coming in twenty minutes. Think about what you want to eat and let me know."

Five, then ten minutes pass, and still she can't decide. "Ten more minutes," you tell her.

"No, I don't want anything."

What do you do?

1. Spend the whole ten minutes nagging, scolding, and trying to strong-arm the child into eating.

2. Sneak a granola bar into her backpack so she'll at least have a snack before lunch.

3. Let her go without breakfast. She's obviously not that hungry right now, and lunch is just a couple hours away.

The best answer is 3, absent some medical condition that makes scheduled meals essential. It's not 1, because it's rarely productive to try to force a child to eat. And it's not 2, because 2 is a bailout, which gives her the message that her actions have no consequences. In adult life, if you're paralyzed with indecision, you're going to miss out on things. That's why 3, painful as it is for a parent, is in fact the most effective option. It places the responsibility to eat on the child, the only one who can fulfill it, and it teaches her an invaluable lesson about the real world. Hunger before lunch is a natural consequence that will probably deter her, from then on, from breakfast indecisiveness.

This is not easy for most parents, myself included. Knowingly allowing your child to suffer a consequence is a real challenge, but the lesson learned is worth the discomfort to both parent and child. And the confidence and pride gained makes it all worthwhile.

In the Morning Madness Game Plan sidebar on page 162, one of the tasks I mention that children can handle on their own is assembling their supplies for school. Think of the skills this task teaches them, like how to organize their possessions and how to anticipate their own needs. They won't develop those capacities—or even focus on remembering what they're supposed to bring—if you take charge of the process. What you want to do is to bolster their self-reliance.

Of course, with a three-year-old, you'll want to discuss the supplies beforehand and perhaps make a final check, asking, "Do you have those pictures you cut out?" But by the time your child gets to kindergarten, just one or two episodes of showing up without her painstakingly done homework will be more of an incentive to stay organized than any degree of nagging.

Teaching children to be accountable helps them to keep track of their possessions. This can be tough, as my chat with my neighbor Judith shows.

> Judith dropped by to ask if by chance my kids had spotted the handheld game player that five-year-old Alex had lost. She said, "I bet he left it at the soccer field. I warned him to leave it home. We searched the field and the bleachers but couldn't find it. I can't imagine where else it could be."

"They didn't mention it," I told her. "I'll be sure to ask them at dinner."

"Alex is miserable," Judith said. "He loves that game! I hate to run out and get him a new one, but I also don't like seeing him so upset."

Judith was right. Running out to replace the device would give Alex the wrong message—that he didn't have to live with consequences of being careless. Without experiencing those consequences, how would he ever learn the value of special possessions? As parents, we do our children a grave disservice if we fulfill their every desire without teaching them respect and gratitude for what they have.

So, not replacing the game player was one very fair, appropriate solution.

Another, I told her, was to have Alex figure out what he would do earn to the replacement. At five, he wasn't getting a substantial allowance, and even if he were, surely it would take ages to recoup the cost. So what was needed was a symbolic gesture, involving an investment of kid-hours by Alex, something that would give him a concrete sense of the worth of the object.

> A couple days later I heard from Judith. "We took your advice and Alex came up with a plan," she told me. "His grandmother said that she has a bunch of shoeboxes of old photos that need to be put into albums. So Alex is going to spend some time there, over the next few weekends, helping her stick them to the pages. He will earn some money for being her personal organizer, so he can buy a new game."

"A brilliant solution!" I said. "How great that he thought it up himself."

And what a great chance to learn about his family's history. But whether or not he enjoyed the task, one thing was for certain: working to replace the game would definitely make him more accountable in the future.

As your child grows older, you'll naturally want to increase the complexity of her chores. Even if you have household help, she needs to have a grasp of such basic skills as keeping the house tidy and sorting and doing her laundry. She should learn to prepare a simple meal or two, even if you live on takeout, and so on. Self-sufficiency is, after all, the foundation of adulthood, and it's our job as parents to foster the skills to help our children achieve it—to make them self-reliant.

The Daily Drill Recap

Here are some at-a-glance, age-appropriate guidelines for transferring responsibilities to kids to help them develop self-reliance.

- **Toddlerhood On: The Basics.** Urge children who can walk well to walk as much as possible; do not carry them unless absolutely necessary. As they approach age three, they can pull their own wheeled backpacks. Once kids start to speak, encourage them to process and articulate thoughts; do not fill in the blanks. Help your children embrace locomotion and communication as pillars of self-reliance.

- **Toddlerhood On: Self-Care.** Supervise tooth brushing and help with face washing (most children can wash their hands by age two). Encourage your children to dress themselves and help them master that skill with kid-friendly, pull-on clothes. Offer children a choice of two outfits, and, for dawdlers, use a kitchen timer or a reward chart to speed up the morning routine.

- **Toddlerhood On: Household Tasks.** Children can and should take responsibility for performing household chores. It's best for kids to perform chores at consistent times, or they're likely to forget. I don't recommend paying kids to pitch in on common household tasks. If they go above and beyond, you can reward them with a special outing or privilege. Do not redo children's chores. If need be, explain constructively (and patiently) how to improve the task. If you redo a child's every effort, you're not teaching responsibility or showing him you have confidence in his ability.

  As kids grow older, their chores should increase in complexity. I don't think any child should graduate from grade school, say, without knowing how to do the laundry or make a meal. If you start early, by the time college rolls around, they will be masters.

- **Four to Six Years On: Accountability.** Introduce accountability—accepting and living with consequences of actions. Don't bail your child out of every difficulty. For personal possessions that are lost or broken, don't step up with immediate replacements. Work with your child to come up with solutions that will promote better care in the future.

CHAPTER 8

Bones of Contention: Conflicts with Siblings and Friends

Three-and-a-half-year-old Nora had been my patient since she was born. When her brother Jonathan, now sixteen months, came along, she wasn't any more upset than most kids. But recently something had changed, according to their mother, Alice.

"Now Jonathan is getting into everything," she said. "It's driving Nora a little wild. She's become superterritorial about her toys and can't bear to have Jonathan touch them. Of course, as soon as she tries to play with something, Jonathan wants it too. It's like I'm always yelling at Nora, demanding that she stop shouting at her brother and warning her not to swat him. I can't yet reason with Jonathan, but it's not really fair to her.

"The other day when he snatched a toy, she threw such a fit that I took it away. I was sure she was going to clobber him. That made Jonathan scream, of course. With the two of them bawling, I was ready to lose my mind. I was about to give Nora a time-out, but she ran off, shrieking, 'I hate him!' and I had to calm Jonathan down.

"And, after all, how many time-outs can you give a kid?

"I know they're supposed to settle disputes themselves, but these conflicts escalate so fast. When they hit the blow-up point, I just have to step in. There's no time to let them work it out on their own."

Sibling rivalry is inevitable, and Alice's experience shows some of the reasons why. A younger child always wants to imitate an older one. A sixteen-month-old, in particular, is hardwired to copy more grownup behavior. The notions that certain toys might belong to his older sister or that it's not his turn to play with them are beyond his understanding.

The older child naturally resents always having to share and to indulge her brother's curiosity, even if she's less possessive with children her own age. With kids at the stages of Alice's, the battle lines are drawn quickly.

As Alice noted, many experts urge parents to allow kids to settle disputes themselves. But that doesn't mean standing idly by until the conflict hits a flashpoint. Instead, it means empowering children to develop independent solutions, intervening in ways that don't involve simply meting out "justice."

It rarely helps when parents stay front and center in conflicts. When Alice scolded Nora, she was likely just stoking the frustration of a preschooler already fed up with a toddler's persistent grabbing. When Alice expressed her annoyance by yelling, understandably, she was probably getting both kids even more riled up. She was modeling the very behavior—shouting when stressed—that she was trying get Nora to stop.

"It sounds like you need to intervene in a different way," I told her. "Nora probably feels helpless, at the mercy of both you and her brother. She needs a more proactive strategy to keep Jonathan at bay. First of all, instead of telling her not to yell, you can give her a positive alternative by asking her what toy she can give to Jonathan to distract him. This empowers her to come up with a solution—a strategy that she can repeat when you're not present. You could also have her choose a few toys that she will always share with Jonathan and others that are strictly hands-off. You make that distinction with toys that she takes to the playground, don't you? Or when other kids are over to play?"

"Pretty much," Alice said. "She knows she can't take anything to the playground that she's not willing to share. It's not as much of an issue when kids her age come over. Mostly they seem to play interactive games, like hide-and-seek or dress-up or fairyland. They don't tend to monopolize toys in quite the same way."

"That makes sense," I said. "Nora could try introducing Jonathan to some of these less toy-oriented games. Little by little, she could also help teach him to share. You should praise her when she figures out ways to play with him without losing her cool—for solving her own problem, with your guidance.

"In the meantime, Jonathan could use stronger, more consistent limits when it comes to bugging his sister. Instead of taking away toys, you could remove him from the scene—not as punishment but to show that him constant grabbing, though he wants to investigate whatever Nora has, is not acceptable. After two minutes, let him come back to give him another chance. It may take a while, but eventually he'll catch on. And it might help Nora feel more understood.

"If you just remove Jonathan calmly, without getting exasperated, that will help keep the kids' tempers down. It's hard to stay calm, but kids tend to react at the same emotional pitch that we do."

Preschoolers, who are developing a sense of fairness, rules, and order, will be provoked when younger siblings take their possessions. These inevitable provocations will be a fine opportunity to introduce your older child to conflict resolution, especially when you ask your older child what he thinks he could do to draw attention away from the toy he wants.

The goal is to guide your child through ways to resolve his own conflicts. By having him brainstorm solutions, you want to empower your child to assert and, ultimately, to fulfill his needs, if possible, though cooperation without adult intervention.

Children usually manage to resolve their own squabbles, but they often need adult guidance, especially when they're at such incompatible developmental points as Nora and Jonathan. A sixteen-month-old wants to lay claim to everything in sight, while a preschooler, who's developing a sense of fairness, rules, and order, will bridle at such "selfishness." Throughout childhood, sibling relationships can grow so fraught that it's hard to imagine that they'll become rewarding when kids grow up. But most of the time, they do.

The New Kid

From the moment your new baby comes home, you can expect sibling rivalry to kick in. The way it's expressed will probably depend on your child's age and temperament. Many children will regress by acting more babyish, wanting a bottle or a diaper, and may get upset or demand immediate attention when you nurse or change the infant. A child who's toilet trained may start having accidents. Some kids will get aggressive, snatching things away from the baby, swatting or tugging him, or roughhousing in a joint expression of jealousy and affection. Obviously, you'll want to supervise older siblings' interactions and teach them to be gentle with the baby.

Paradoxically, you can help older children to adjust, not by babying them but by empowering them with more "big-kid" responsibilities. To underscore their "big-kid" status—and to show that it doesn't mean losing attention and affection—spend some "alone" time each day with the older sibling, doing things, like coloring together or playing a game, that are too grown-up for the baby.

It helps to prepare your older child by sharing your excitement during your pregnancy. Young toddlers won't really understand what's coming, but as an introduction, you can read stories about babies and show them their own baby pictures. Both boys and girls may like having their own "babies"—dolls—to practice playing with and nurturing. If you involve kids in shopping for baby things and setting up the nursery, they'll feel a part of the welcoming process.

Once the baby arrives, even a very young toddler may enjoy taking charge of a baby-related task—say, handing you a diaper when you're changing the baby. You might ask her to pat the baby gently or talk to him sweetly when he cries. She may like amusing the baby by singing or making funny faces. When the baby responds by smiling or gurgling, she'll be delighted, a feeling that you can reinforce by praising her for being such a fun sibling. Preschoolers will feel empowered if you ask them to make decisions, like "Which song should we sing together for the baby?" or "What color would the baby like to wear today?"

Of course, some children would rather ignore the new sibling for a while. If that's the case with your older child, don't push it. Be supportive and loving. In time, all kids come around and accept the new kid—until they start squabbling, that is.

The Squall Factor I

It's easy to attribute the clashes between Jonathan and Nora to their respective developmental stages. But, as most parents can attest, siblings don't need much of reason to butt heads. The underlying cause of many sibling squalls is competition for parental attention, but plenty seem to spring from simple one-upmanship.

> Monica's two kids, Samantha and Ethan, were ages three and five, respectively. "They'll fight about anything," she said. "Last night, you wouldn't believe what set them off. They both wanted the same seat at the dinner table!
>
> "I mean, who cares? It's not like either one offers a view of the Grand Canyon. But one is closer to the window, and they've apparently decided that's the 'good' seat. They'd been bickering all day, so I guess this was just the latest battle."

"What did you do?" I asked.

"Well, I yelled at them to just sit in the nearest chair. As you can imagine, Ethan plunked down and then Samantha tried to climb all over him. He shouted and shoved her, and she fell on the floor, shrieking. So I made Ethan move and put Samantha in that chair. Ethan cried and sulked throughout the whole meal.

"Now I feel guilty. Ethan pushed Samantha, which he knows is wrong. But she was the one who climbed on him and probably instigated the fight."

Monica's dilemma is all too common. Even if parents actually witness an angry outburst, it can be hard to know what provoked it. That's why I told Monica, "My default position is usually, 'It takes two to tango.'"

Getting in the middle of the squabble and trying to sort out competing cries of "He did this!" and "But she said this!" or, like Monica, simply imposing a sanction on the child who seems aggressive, may not resolve the immediate dispute—which, in any case, might be fairly trivial. It doesn't teach children that behavior in any given moment is part of a bigger picture.

The real issue in this situation wasn't who deserved the "good" seat, but the fact that both kids were disrupting the family dinner, the time in the day reserved for enjoying one another's company. By "settling" the dispute, Monica didn't solve that issue, since the dinner was marred by Ethan's bad temper. Her resolution also did nothing to teach the kids to negotiate and share in the future.

A more instructive and far-reaching, "big-picture" response, I explained, would have been to say, "Your fighting is disrupting our dinner hour. Both of you go to your rooms so we can eat in peace. And while you're there, think about how to choose who gets the 'good seat,' tonight and from now on. Are you going to take turns or come up with some other plan?

"When we're done eating, we'll call you. Then you two can have dinner by yourselves."

I often recommended this strategy to parents in my practice, and I've used it in my own home when sibling storms threaten family harmony. It's very effective because it transcends the specifics of most battles. Without taking sides, parents can curtail unacceptable behavior quickly and give the squabblers a needed chance to cool down. If guidance is necessary, parents can offer it later, when children are less fired up and more able to be receptive.

It also delivers an important big-picture message: to participate in family life, kids have to keep the peace rather than browbeat each other to get what they want or lash out at every real or imagined slight. By removing kids from the parents' presence, it encourages them to negotiate disagreements and to satisfy their desires independently. It makes them self-reliant.

The Playdate Protocol sidebar on page 192 describes other strategies that work as well for sibling conflicts as they do squabbles with friends. The Age-Appropriate Boundaries sidebar on page 184 offers some thoughts on handling the times when squabbling takes an aggressive turn.

Without adults in the equation, the schemes children devise to settle their differences can be wonderfully inventive. I saw this with my own kids one snowy afternoon.

To keep them occupied indoors, I'd bought a set of make-your-own-animation books. In two of the books, the outlines were already drawn and ready to be colored in.

After coloring, you could flip the pages in one and watch a caterpillar become a butterfly; in the second, a tadpole became a frog. The other two books were blank, so you could draw your own progressive images and flip the pages to watch them change.

Right away, there was trouble. I'd barely left the room when I heard squabbling and then, "Mom . . . "

I stuck my head back in. "I picked the tadpole first!" my daughter claimed. "But as soon as I said that, he grabbed it."

My son was clutching the book to his chest, as she tried to wrestle it away. He was swatting and pushing at her hands.

"Look, you two," I told them. "These books are supposed to be fun. If you can't enjoy them, I'm going to take them away. That means no grabbing, no hitting, no fighting. You need to use your words to figure out what to do."

Then I left them alone. When I returned, they were working quietly. "Look what we decided," my daughter said. "I'm tracing the tadpole pages in the blank book. That way, we can both do it."

"What a great solution," I said. "I never would have thought of that."

I congratulated both kids for the ingenious plan and for playing together so nicely. I gave my son special kudos for waiting patiently for his sister to finish—delaying gratification isn't easy for a four-year-old—and both on the spot and later, when we were alone, I praised my daughter effusively for doing the tracing so her brother could color the design he wanted. I was so proud of her kindness, and, importantly, I could see that she was proud of herself.

Age-Appropriate Boundaries

Aggressive behavior is developmentally normal in toddlers and pre-schoolers. But *aggressive* is a big umbrella, describing everything from roughhousing and shoving to out-and-out bullying. How do parents reconcile children's very real need to fight their own battles with the imperative of protecting them from harm?

It's tempting to rush in and intervene at every sign of squawking. But such a scattershot approach does little to discourage aggressive behavior over the long term. It's far more effective—and less confusing for children—to set firm, age-appropriate boundaries between toler-able and unacceptable behavior and to enforce them consistently. The disciplinary methods described in chapter 6 can help enforce them.

What are some examples of age-appropriate boundaries?

- **Toddlers.** At this age, children don't have much control over their emotional impulses and are just developing the verbal skills to articulate how they're feeling. So, when frustrated, they often lash out by screaming, kicking, and hitting. When they act out in this way with other children, immediately but calmly remove them from the scene. Apply the strategies from the Stormy Weather sidebar on page 140. Urge them to use their words to express their frustration.

  But what about behavior like biting, spitting, and hair pulling? Many children go through a biting phase, sometimes because they're teething. Giving them something else to chew on can help. Spitting and hair pulling are often attention-getting ploys, ones that are quite effective at getting a scream out of a sibling. Telling the child, "We don't [bite, spit, pull hair]" underscores the fact that such behavior is unacceptable, though repeated removals may be needed to get the point across. It's worth suggesting that the sibling not overreact to the behavior, explaining that a big fuss may be just what the toddler wants. It can also help if the sibling understands that the toddler is probably not acting maliciously but simply trying to provoke a reaction.

- **Preschoolers/Kindergartners.** Aggression declines somewhat in the preschool years, as children's verbal and social skills improve. By preschool and kindergarten age, children respond more readily to the disciplinary actions described in chapter 6 as they grow aware that aggression has consequences. Now there's more shoving and swatting instead of spitting and biting.

How much of this you're willing to tolerate is a personal choice. Parents of multiple boys, especially, seem to get inured to a degree of roughhousing that many of us would find daunting.

Obviously, it's not normal if a preschooler frequently strikes out in anger or does so violently enough to hurt another child. In such cases, you should consult your pediatrician. But no matter how well you parent, there will be times when your preschooler or kindergartner's frustration erupts in a physical reaction. When this happens, you'll want to explore the reasons and verbal alternatives with the child, as well as take disciplinary action.

A common child's alternative to aggressive modes of retaliation is tattling. Tattling does have an upside. A child who tattles is showing respect for the behavioral guidelines you've established— well enough to inform on a sibling or playmate who's crossed the line. And, of course, when safety is at stake, you want to stress that your child must immediately come to you for help.

The downside is that plenty of tattling is aimed at currying favor or making trouble for an annoying sibling or friend. It allows your child to avoid having to settle his own disputes— the lessons you've been working so hard to instill. Once you've determined that nothing dangerous is going on, you can turn that responsibility back to the tattler by asking, "What can you do solve this problem? What can you say that might make a difference?"

The tattler will recognize that he actually does know how to resolve at least some of his disputes, which will boost his self-reliance.

Fair Share

By the time a child is around three, the intense self-absorption of toddlerhood begins to wane. Though it will take most kids a while to gain the cognitive capacity to put themselves fully in another person's shoes, at three they start showing glimmerings of empathy that grow stronger throughout the preschool years. By six, my daughter's age at the time of the animation book incident, you'd expect to see a well-developed capacity to share and a fair degree of empathy, though I was still proud of her conflict resolution.

When a very young child who is, say, eating a cookie or piece of toast holds it up to offer you a bite, she's more likely mimicking adult behavior than actually trying to share. While it's not realistic to expect kids this young to grasp the concept of sharing, you can model the behavior so it comes more easily later on. Most children don't reach that point, developmentally, until they're between two and three years old.

Instilling Empathy and Willingness to Share

Around the age of two or three years old, you can begin to instill empathy, along with the willingness to share, in your child by incorporating the following into your daily life.

Taking Turns. You can make sharing fun by taking turns when playing with your child. If you're helping him assemble the track for a toy train, you can alternate attaching pieces; once it's put together, you can trade off pushing different cars, like the engine and the caboose. When you read a book together, you can turn a page, and then ask him if he'd like to turn the next one. If he's blowing bubbles, you can ask for the chance to try your hand with the wand—make it a game to alternate back and forth. In the sandbox, you can "borrow" the shovel and pail. If you're coloring or drawing together, you can switch off using crayons, asking explicitly, "May I have a turn using the red? You can use the blue, and then we'll trade back."

It's easy to build taking turns into many activities, to accustom your child to the fact that it's an essential element of social life.

Asking Permission. In the examples above, you'll note that getting your turn can involve asking permission. You show your child that you respect his property by asking before you, say, grab the purple crayon when coloring or the coal car when playing with a toy train. That may be just what he wants to use, and he should always be allowed to say no. Then you can ask, "Which one would you like me to have?" and let him decide. Let him reserve a few special things that no one else gets to play with, with the understanding that others are to be shared.

Why ask permission? By making it the child's choice to share, you're letting him feel satisfaction at doing something for others rather than stew in resentment of a stricture that you've imposed. It's a mode of interaction that you're trying to teach him to perform independently, because it feels good. Ideally, the lesson will be reinforced when other kids share with him in turn.

Furthermore, requesting permission distinguishes *asking* him to give you something from *telling* him to give you something. For example, if he's playing with matches, you aren't going to *ask* him but rather *tell* him to hand them over—and expect him to do it promptly.

When he does share, thank and praise him. Model the kind of courteous give-and-take that you want him to have with others.

Encouraging Cooperation. Taking turns is not a perfect science. When siblings play, you'll probably observe that one tends to dominate and to get his way much of the time. Tempting though it may be, don't step in to rectify the inequity by saying, "Ricky, you always get to go first. Now it should be Gabe's turn."

Instead, hang back a while to see if the kids manage to balance out their relationship. It's important that Gabe learn to assert himself, rather than have you fight his battles, when playing with someone who's too controlling. Eventually, he'll get fed up and say, "No fair!'

Often the older child rules the roost, but don't be surprised if it's the younger one who gets too pushy. It can be a matter of temperament, the children's stages of development—around four, many kids enter a bossy phase—or simply the fact that the older sibling is more practiced at self-restraint.

If you feel that you must intervene because one child is too painfully frustrated or the other just too overwhelming, do so out of the moment. Talk to the dominant child privately, without scolding. You can say, "Your brother loves you so much. When I see you play, he always gives in because he wants you to be happy. But don't you think it would be nice, once in a while, to let him choose the game or movie or to let him go first? Can you think of a time when you can give him that chance? Or can you think of a fair way to decide who gets to choose?"

Also talk to the nondominant child, planting a similar suggestion. Try saying something like "You're so nice to your brother, always letting him go first and choose the movies and games. But I bet there are times when you wish you could get your way. Can you think of a plan that will let you do that sometimes?"

By encouraging cooperation in this way, you're giving children essential negotiating tools to manage their relationships. You won't always be there to keep everything fair and square.

Thinking Aloud. Articulate your interpretations of others' feelings and encourage your child to do the same. If another child cries when it's time to leave the playground, you might say, "I wonder if he's hungry or tired. Or maybe he just doesn't want to go home. What do you think?"

Get him in the habit of considering what other people might be feeling, and show him that you're sensitive to his state of mind. You can say, "It seems like you are feeling sad. Is it because you have so much fun at Grandma's that you don't want to leave? Or is it something else? "

In this way you can both stimulate and model empathetic thinking.

Displaying Generosity and Sharing. Offer your child a bite of your dessert. Let him look at your smart phone. Hand him your sunglasses when he wants to try them on. Use the word *share* to characterize these actions, and also when you offer things to others, as in, "I'm going to *share* this sandwich with Aunt Debbie." Your example is always the best teacher for your child.

The Squall Factor II

In our own homes, with our own children, we can teach civility and cooperation. We cannot control what other parents or their kids do, for better or for worse. The following anecdote describes a challenging parent-child dynamic.

"What would you do if this happened?" Lori asked. "I took Megan to the playground, where a boy was playing with water balloons, filling them up at the fountain, and then throwing them so they'd pop on the ground. He was a little older than Megan—maybe four or five.

"We've never had anything like that in our house, so she was fascinated with the balloons. We'd play for a while, and then I'd sit on the bench while she went to watch the kid throw and pop them. Finally, she got up the nerve to ask if she could try it too. She asked a few times, but the kid kept saying no. His mother, who was sitting right there, didn't seem to care. She never said a word.

"Finally, poor Megan burst into tears and said, 'You have to share!'

"I picked up Megan to comfort her, and I got mad. 'Who brings water balloons to a playground and doesn't share them?' I asked the mother.

"She sort of shrugged and said, 'Why can't your kid play with her own toys?'

"I walked away with Megan, and then we went home. I mean, why bother to teach our kids the right values when parents like that promote brattiness? I hardly knew what to say to Megan, except for 'I'm sorry that boy was mean.' I bought her a popsicle as consolation."

I could certainly understand Lori's feelings—and who knows? Had I been there, I might have shared them. I could understand that her reaction sprung from natural protective instincts. But this surely wouldn't be the only time that Megan would encounter unkindness and disappointment. If we could, we'd protect our kids from unhappiness for their entire lives. But since that's not possible, the best we can do is use such moments to offer lessons.

What lessons was Lori teaching here? That Megan was ineffectual at getting what she wanted and needed Lori to fight for her? That the other child was mean and wrong? That the other mother deserved a scolding? That when you're disappointed you get a popsicle?

The trouble with these "lessons" is that they're all dead ends. They don't help the child process the "mean" behavior or help her cope with disappointment in the future. They also don't acknowledge Megan's accomplishment of behaving appropriately—not grabbing a balloon or fighting for it, but asking nicely. Even if her hopes were dashed, she deserved credit for that. Instead, Lori's outburst—which did nothing to gain Megan a balloon—became the dominant feature of the incident.

So, here's what I told Lori:

"I would have gone over to support Megan, too. But I might not have picked her up right away, since she wasn't hurt but disappointed. I might have waited to see how the other child responded to Megan's words. She may have been convincing, and if she was down on his level, she might have gotten a balloon. The kids may have engaged constructively together.

"If that didn't happen soon and Megan was still distressed, I would have tried to distract her by leading her to another part of the playground. I would have comforted her, saying, 'I'm so sorry that you were disappointed. Sharing is the rule in our house, and you're really good about it. But not all kids learn that lesson at the same time. Maybe that boy doesn't understand sharing yet. Maybe he needs more practice playing with other children. Why do think he wouldn't share?'

continued on page 194

Playdate Protocol

Entertaining friends is a thrilling milestone for your child. At preschool age, kids begin to take genuine pride in sharing their homes, families, and belongings with other children. The pride they develop comes from welcoming friends into their warm, comfortable environment.

Of course, when children get together, conflicts are inevitable. Here are some ways to help playdates run smoothly while encouraging independent play:

- **Accompany your child or invite other parents to your home** on the first few playdates children have. Getting to know the parents is an important safety measure, of course, but it will also give you a sense of their values and how they interact with children. Your presence in the beginning will also help your child feel more secure.

- **Put away the toys that your child doesn't like to share** before the guest arrives.

- **Limit the time for playdates to an hour at first.** Overstimulated or worn-out kids are a prescription for conflict.

- **Make it clear that you're readily available to both kids** without micromanaging them. You can say, "I'll be here at my desk, working on some papers, but either of you can come and get me if you want."

- **Don't criticize, yell at, or punish a visiting child,** if play gets inappropriate. That can be too frightening. You can give your own child a time-out, if necessary, but your best recourses when playdate trouble flares are limiting setting, redirection, and guidance (or a combination), without laying blame.

Limit Setting. If a visitor is violating your house rules, like throwing a ball indoors, simply remove it. You can say, "We only play with balls outdoors. What else would you like to do?" If a visitor gets aggressive, you can lay down the law calmly: "We don't hit in this house; we use words. Can you tell my daughter what you want?"

Redirection. If a visitor wants to play a game or watch a movie that you think is too violent or otherwise inappropriate, don't editorialize, since his parents might allow it. You can say, "That's not a game [movie] that we play [watch]" or "I'm not familiar with that movie [game]. I'd rather see you pick out something else."

Guidance. Encourage verbal expression of likes and dislikes: "Would you like to tell our visitor your favorite games?" "Let's ask our visitor his favorite colors."

If children don't seem able to resolve their differences, ask—don't tell—them what to do. This strategy can be helpful if either child comes in to tattle on the other.

The other child may be used to having parents solve conflicts rather than come up with solutions. You can say, "Let's all talk. What do you think would solve this problem? What are your ideas?"

- When you check in on the kids, praise them both for playing nicely, giving specifics: "I love how you're taking turns being the mommy"; "You figured out such a good way to share those cars"; "You both use your words so well."

- Recap the playdate for the other child's parents, noting what they did, what conflicts arose, and how the kids (or you, if that proved necessary) handled them.

continued from page 191

"I definitely would have praised her for asking nicely for a balloon, saying, 'That was so grown up. It made me proud. Now, let's think of something else we could play with that's really fun. What do you feel like doing?'

"My strategy might not have consoled her, of course, but my aim would have been to give her some satisfaction— at least the confirmation that her independent actions were correct. I would have tried to honor her self-reliance."

When our children squabble with siblings, we can handle the situation with "big-picture" solutions, addressing both opponents' behavior, aimed at teaching them to resolve their disputes independently. When they clash with other children, including their friends, we may need different approaches. The goal is the same—to empower children to assert their needs and to fulfill them, if possible, though cooperation, without adult intervention. But it can get more complicated.

Why—and how—we discipline our children is deeply personal. Some parents will say to other parents, "If my kid acts up at your house, you have free rein. I trust you." Others feel uncomfortable delegating the task of discipline. Obviously, if play gets rough, you have to intervene to protect your child, but the Playdate Protocol sidebar on page 192 offers some strategies for peaceful resolution.

The lessons of this chapter—how to assert yourself, how to cooperate, how to reach peaceful resolutions independently, without outside intervention—may test parents' mettle, but they are lifelong gifts for our kids. They are the building blocks of self-reliance.

Bones of Contention Recap

Here are some at-a-glance strategies to help kids of various ages learn to resolve disputes with siblings and friends.

- **Two to Three Years.** Instill empathy and willingness to share. Take turns when you play with your children, ask permission (to make it clear that sharing is the child's choice), and model sharing and empathy.

- **Three to Four Years.** Practice sharing, taking turns, and feeling empathy. Guide your child in brainstorming solutions to resolve conflicts.

- **Four to Six Years.** Encourage your children to resolve conflicts with siblings and friends. Apply a "big-picture" strategy, transcending the specifics of any given fight—for example, emphasize the need for a peaceful home. Ask your child, "What could you say that might make a difference in this situation?"

CHAPTER 9

Give and Take: Problem Solving and Decision Making

Five-year-old Stevie was teary-eyed as he sat with his mother in my exam room. In each hand, he held a piece of plastic. "Look," he said.

"That's his yo-yo," his mother, Nancy, told me. "It lights up, and it's his new favorite toy. He was flinging it around in the parking lot, and it smacked against the building and broke."

"Oh no," I said.

"I'm sorry, Stevie, but toys are made to be used a certain way," Nancy said. "You were swinging it like a lasso, not a yo-yo. Didn't I tell you not to be rough with it?"

She shook her head, turning to me. "I hate to get him a new one. It's not the money—it's that he just doesn't listen."

"Well, you could make this a lesson," I said. "I wouldn't run right out to replace it."

"You wouldn't?"

"He could replace it out of his allowance, or he could fix it."

"Fix it!" Stevie wailed.

"How would you fix it?" I asked.

He looked around, sniffling, until he spotted the cellophane tape dispenser on my desk. "Tape!" he exclaimed.

"Good idea," I said. "Why don't you use this special strong tape?"

I took a roll of bandage tape out of my drawer and gave to him. He struggled, trying to pry up the cut end. Thrusting the tape at his mother, he whined, "Fix it!"

"No, Stevie, you can do it," I said. I peeled up the edge of the tape and handed it back to him.

As his mother and I chatted, Stevie was laboriously unwinding the tape and wrapping it around the yo-yo. An adult could have done it in seconds, but that wasn't the point.

When he finished, he stood up to try the yo-yo. It looked a bit lumpy. But, he said excitedly, "It works!"

While tales of broken toys and distraught children are certainly commonplace, it's scenarios like this one that raise some very important parenting questions about fostering your child's sense of self-reliance. What if Nancy had stopped on the way home and bought Stevie a new yo-yo?

He would have concluded, and rightly so, that his mother's words were meaningless—that if he got rough and broke something, she would simply replace it as if nothing had happened. In other words, his ill-advised actions would have no consequences. He would have no compelling reason to take care of his possessions. Why bother? His parents would readily supply anything he wanted. Clearly, these are not the lessons we want to teach our kids.

Now, think about what Stevie actually learned from the experience.

First of all, he got concrete evidence, in the form of a broken yo-yo, that it was worth paying attention to his mother. He learned that if he didn't pay attention, there would be a consequence: losing a toy that he really enjoyed. But by coming up with a way to fix the yo-yo, he recognized his own capacity to construct solutions to problems, and by doing the repair himself, he learned to implement those solutions. He discovered that he could be self-reliant.

This is a major discovery that deserves to be reinforced.

What do you do when your child has, say, a motorized car that stops running? He brings it to you in frustration. For many of us, the inclination is to simply replace the batteries and hand it back to the child. But, even with very young children, it pays to talk through the steps that remedy the situation aloud, so the child can hear how you solve problems. By the time he's three or four, don't tell, but ask him what might be wrong with the car. Help him diagnose the toy as having dead batteries.

He can even bring you the package of replacement batteries to solve the problem. **Safety Note:** Button batteries are dangerous if swallowed, so make sure that your child knows that supervision is required when handling them and that spent ones must be discarded properly.

The point is to suppress the reflex most of us have to handle every challenging situation for our kids. In chapter 7, we discussed the self-care and household responsibilities that children can readily assume from toddlerhood on, if adults step back and allow it. Taking charge of daily routines and household jobs gives kids a great sense of competence. Taking charge fosters self-reliance.

In this chapter, I urge parents to boost kids' self-reliance by recognizing teachable moments—chances, like the ones just described, for them to solve their own problems. Developing the ability to assess a situation and then deciding how best to approach it is an essential life skill. As kids test out the approaches they've come up with, they begin to refine their instincts for what works and what doesn't. They learn to trust themselves. By encouraging this kind of independent thinking and testing rather than automatically stepping in, we empower them to face challenges and to make good choices. We instill self-reliance.

Child Support

Letting kids solve their own problems doesn't mean simply abandoning them to sink or swim. It means being present to guide and support them, if necessary, but not to spring instantly to the rescue. It means reinforcing, not undermining, their sense of their own capability. Let's look at a more challenging situation than a broken toy.

> A three-year-old who loves to climb has reached the platform at the top of a particularly large piece of playground equipment. Once there, she's unsure that she wants to try

the corkscrew slide, which is the easiest way down. So she sits on the platform, watching other kids slide. She's not crying, but clearly she's hesitant. You were already biting your nails, watching her climb.

So, now what do you do?

1. Panic. Call the fire department to come with a cherry picker.

2. Climb up yourself. When you reach her, you'll decide how to get her down.

3. Wait it out. She'll eventually screw up the nerve to go down the slide once she sees how much the other kids enjoy it.

4. Point out how much fun other kids are having on the side and attempt to talk her into trying it.

5. Ask her if she's ready to come down. If so, ask her how she plans to do it, while offering to "spot" her—to stand by to catch her if she needs help.

Tempting though it may be, 1 is obviously the wrong solution. Option 2 is very hard for most parents to resist. But unless there's a compelling safety reason—in which case you must act—or the child's truly distraught, it's wise not to rush right in to save the day. Doing so will reinforce your child's fear, confirming that she can't function without you. You're telling her, "You're not competent"—a very discouraging message. Getting stuck at the top is her problem, not yours, and she deserves the chance to solve it, bolstered by your faith.

Option 4 may seem encouraging, but it's really the flip side of option 2. It's you deciding how the child should solve the problem and trying to convince her to do it your way. You might prevail—and she might even discover that she loves the slide—but the goal is not to push her to be brave. Why make her self-conscious about her fear, if that's what's holding her back?

Option 3 is not a solution but a temporary holding pattern. It's worth giving her time to watch the other kids and consider what she wants to do. But the slide is not the only way to get down.

That leaves 5, which to my mind is the most empowering option. It honors your child's fear without validating the idea that she has reason to be more afraid than other kids, who have no problem sliding. It shows that you trust her instincts; if she's not ready to go on the slide, so be it. She'll have plenty of other chances.

Importantly, option 5 lets her determine that there are several solutions to the problem. Once she realizes that, she can puzzle through them to find one that she can comfortably attempt. If need be, you can explore them with her, saying, "You climbed up on the parallel bars. That's one way to get down. Do you see some other ways?" It also affirms that you will support her in her choice by "spotting" her to make sure that she doesn't fall.

If her choice is, "Mommy, come get me!" you can reply, "I know you can figure out a way to solve this problem. Take a moment to think about it."

If she's stuck in her fear, you can guide her with a few suggestions, but ultimately it's best to let her take ownership of the solution. If she's really at a loss and paralyzed with terror, you can point out the easiest way down or make your way up to get her. However, the next time she wants to climb the thing, be sure to discuss the fact that going up means figuring out how to get down.

It does make a big difference, in this situation, if being rescued is her idea, not just the automatic flexing of your parental muscles. Letting her take the lead shows her that the best first line of attack, for any problem, is to consider her possibilities for solving it—even if her ultimate solution is looking to a parent for help. It shows her that she can be self-reliant.

The Friend Zone

Many of the situations from which we feel moved to rescue our children are social. The impulse to do so is natural, of course—we'd love to spare our kids disappointment and bruised feelings. Our first inclination is to rush to their defense, whether they need it or not. That's how Marilyn, the mother of my five-year-old patient Maddie, felt when her daughter was excluded from a birthday party.

> Marilyn could hardly contain her annoyance. "Can you believe it?" she said. "This morning another girl asked Maddie what she was getting their classmate for her birthday. The kid's having a party, and Maddie wasn't invited. What kind of school allows that? All the kids should be invited."
>
> "The kid's not Maddie's best friend, but she's been at our house a few times. Now Maddie feels left out. I want to check with parents I know to see which kids were invited, or call the party hosts and ask if Maddie can come."
>
> "Hmm. . . ." I said. "I'm not sure those sound like positive steps. If Maddie feels bad, surely you can help her deal with it. Involving other parents could have repercussions that would make her feel worse. Your being upset might boost her disappointment, too."

As we talked, Marilyn calmed down. She decided to explain to Maddie that she understood why Maddie felt sad and that even mommies feel sad when they don't get invited to parties. She would leave it to Maddie to ask the other child about it, if that's what she wanted to do, and, if needed, offer guidance.

As it turned out, Maddie did bring up the party with the birthday girl, who said, "I really wanted to invite you on my birthday. But my grandparents and all my cousins are coming, so my mom said I could only pick two friends to ask. Next time I want to have a kids' party."

"Maddie understood that," Marilyn told me. She was even happier when her friend asked her over for a one-on-one playdate. "She feels fine now. It was so much better for the kids to talk than for me to get involved."

Had Marilyn followed through on her helicoptering impulse, she probably would have created plenty of ill will—upsetting parents whose kids weren't invited and may not have known about the party and offending the parents of the birthday girl, who never intended the party to be for classmates. But leaving aside whatever pots she might have stirred—and the fact that she jumped to conclusions, as we all do at times—the real moral of this story is that a child who's disappointed doesn't necessarily need to be rescued.

Disappointments in life are inevitable. There's no way that we can ever completely shield our children—nor should we. The resilience that sustains us in life is often born of disappointment.

Yes, it's painful to weather a seeming snub early on in school, but it's easier to recover and to start to develop a thicker skin than it is to handle a bigger problem later on, without some experience of bouncing back. The loving support and empathy of parents can cushion the blow. Supporting a child by helping her emotionally process the hurt—and, when possible, steering her toward ways to resolve the problem herself—is usually a more powerful antidote than forceful parental intervention.

Marilyn was providing support to Maddie in telling her that she understood why her feelings were hurt and giving her the message that she trusted Maddie, even at her young age, to work out her disappointment on her own. Empowered by that support, Maddie got over her hurt enough to initiate a talk with the birthday girl and, independently, clear up the misunderstanding and maintain their friendship. She learned self-reliance.

Another option is not to directly intervene, as Marilyn planned to do, but to handle children's problems from behind the scenes. Kate, a mother I know from preschool, described a situation that shows how such offstage micromanagement can backfire.

> Kate is one of those of those rare, lucky parents whose kids come home and give her a recap of the day. On occasion, she's actually surprised me with information— nothing earthshaking, but interesting tidbits of who-said-what, which kids are new best friends, and so on. One day at drop-off, she mentioned a difficulty that Jason, her four-year-old son, was having that week with another classmate, David.
>
> "When they play outside, David hogs the swing," she told me. "Jason loves to swing, so that really bugs him. It's also a matter of principle for him, since he's very big on taking turns. I've always been strict with him and his sister about that. If they both want something, I give them

each a certain length of time with it and then they have to switch. I guess David's parents don't enforce taking turns."

"Hmm. . . ." I said. "How's Jason handling it?"

"Well, Monday, I told him to ask David nicely to give him a turn. David kept saying, 'Not yet' and 'Pretty soon.' So poor Jason kept hanging around, waiting for the swing and getting frustrated. Finally, when he turned his back for a minute, David hopped off. But then it was almost time to go inside."

"Poor Jason," I said.

"So, Tuesday, I told him to run out and grab the swing before David got to it. He didn't make it, unfortunately. David is bigger and faster. He's not a bad kid, but I think he's teasing Jason.

"Yesterday, I told Jason to say, firmly, 'David, your time is up!' David sort of laughed at him, and Jason started crying. So today I'm having him tell the teacher to make David give him a turn."

Kate was just chatting, not asking for advice. But if she were, I would have offered some observations. It struck me that Jason might not be very well equipped to handle a teaser like David. He didn't have much practice at asserting himself and resolving conflicts on his own. By Kate's account, she controlled the processes of sharing and taking turns at home rather than having her kids reach agreement by engaging in a typical sibling tug-of-war.

So, from the outset, he was a step or two behind the kids who'd spent more time down in the trenches, working out conflicts with siblings and friends. No wonder he was confused when David didn't surrender the swing when his turn should have been over. At home, he and his sister relied on Kate to allot them each time for a turn.

Also, when Jason was trying to get David off the swing, he didn't have a repertoire of battle-tested strategies. Instead, he was parroting lines that Kate fed him when he described the latest installment of the David struggle. When those lines didn't work, he didn't have a fallback position or the confidence to dream up an entirely new strategy without consulting Kate.

Kate was being supportive to a point in that she heard Jason out and empathized with his distress. But to me—hearing the story secondhand from Kate—it seemed that her offstage micromanagement was not empowering Jason to solve the problem, teaching him self-reliance, but was instead reinforcing his sense of helplessness.

How could she have guided him more effectively?

Problem-Solving Reset

It's not too late to reset and redirect if your natural instinct up until now has been to solve your children's problems for them. It may take time to get them on track, but with some coaxing and encouragement, they'll start to take the initiative. The place to begin is with your own reaction when a problem crops up. Rather than storm right in with the solution, try taking these steps:

- **Pause.** Give yourself a moment to think before tackling the problem.

- **Empathize.** Show your child that you understand her disappointment.

- **Ask Questions.** For example, say, "Hmm. . . . Can you think of different ways to solve this problem? How many can you come up with?"

Rather than tell him what to do or say, she could have asked questions to stimulate his thinking on ways to negotiate with David. For example, when he asked nicely for a turn on the swing and David said, "Not yet," what could he have done instead of hanging around and waiting? Kate wasn't there, so she couldn't suggest it, but if Jason was in the habit of trying to solve his own problems, he might have noticed other classmates doing something fun. He could have joined them and had a good time, feeling less deprived at losing the swing to David and also less victimized. David would have been left swinging by himself, with no onlooker to tease. It's likely that, without an audience, he wouldn't have enjoyed monopolizing the swing.

- **Be Patient.** Children who aren't used to thinking for themselves, especially during times of conflict, will have a hard time processing the problem to the point of reaching a solution. So, give your child time to think. You can even offer a few outlandish solutions to get her mind working and to lighten the mood.

- **Work with Your Child.** If in the beginning your child can't come up with even a single solution, try offering her a few practical ideas. Then let her choose. The choice will give her partial responsibility for the resolution, which is a step in the right direction. With time and practice, she will take full ownership of such conflicts and grow more self-reliant.

The key to this solution's effectiveness would be Jason spotting a second-best activity, with more congenial classmates. Only he could have determined what that activity might be. That's why Kate's well-meaning coaching missed the mark, keeping her son locked in an uncomfortable standoff with David.

Or perhaps David and Jason could have negotiated, settling on a set amount of time for a turn. The teacher could have served as the "stop watch," making sure they each got their agreed-upon minutes. Alternatively, they could have come up with a system of switching off going first each day. The point is that Jason would have been more determined to come up with a comfortable solution if he was the one doing the problem solving, not Kate.

Once our children are past toddlerhood, our physical presence in their daily lives inevitably diminishes with each passing year. They can tell us about the challenges they face, but unless we're actually on the scene, like it or not, we can't really resolve them. That's why we owe it to our kids to empower them to think for themselves and to brainstorm solutions to tough situations, independently, from an early age. The Problem-Solving Reset sidebar on page 206 offers some empowering strategies.

Some of the problems kids face involve their treatment of other children. I got an earful one day when I was driving the carpool.

At recess, a bunch of kids would play wall ball. Most of them were around five or six years old. One of the boys, Jeffrey, was a little younger, smaller, and less coordinated— not that the others were exactly world-class athletes: Most kids don't have the motor skills to start being really good at sports until kindergarten age. So the rules of games can fall by the wayside, especially when kids get excited.

But Jeffrey loved being around the bigger kids, and he was determined to play. None of them wanted to let him. "He's no good," one of the kids was complaining. "He hits the ball before it bounces."

"Yeah, or he catches it," another chimed in. "Ms. Davis makes us play with him. Or else he'll cry."

"Yeah, like a baby."

"He's a big stupid baby. . . ."

Obviously, the intervention by Ms. Davis, the teacher's aide, wasn't doing Jeffrey much good. And, clearly, the conversation I was overhearing needed redirection.

"Guys, what do you think would help him get better?" I asked.

"A new brain!"

"Hmm. . . . I'd love hear a practical suggestion, one that could work."

There was muttering in the backseat. Finally, one of the boys piped up, "I bet if he practiced after school, he could remember the rules better."

"Good idea," I said. "How could he practice?"

"Someone would have to play with him."

After some debate, two volunteers emerged, who were to meet up with Jeffrey at one of their homes to try coaching him. I praised all the boys lavishly for such creative thinking and also for being kind.

The fact that the kids hatched this solution themselves made it likely to work out. An adult demanding that they help Jeffrey, like Ms. Davis making them include him in games, would have probably sparked resistance or, at best, half-hearted and whiny compliance. But now the two volunteers, especially, had a vested interest in seeing Jeffrey get better at the game. The rest of the kids in the car grew more willing to let him play, if only to see how he was improving with coaching. He became more of a pupil for the boys than the outsider that he had been.

That the boys were being kind instead of dismissive is gratifying for adults, but the notions of compassion and inclusion are still somewhat abstract for five- and six-year-olds. Kindness, for all of us and especially children, is often best learned by doing. Jeffrey's appreciation when he was no longer ostracized as "no good" would give the boys empirical evidence of the value of kindness, as would the praise they got from adults. Those factors would teach them a more indelible lesson, at their age, than any lecture about "doing the right thing."

As these examples show, brainstorming solutions to problems and trying them out is a powerful confidence builder for children, giving them a sense of competence and pride. Even if those solutions don't work, helping to refine them offers parents great opportunities to model their own approaches to problems and to coping with disappointment.

Furthermore, working through solutions with your child will show that she can trust you. Had Marilyn called and expressed her upset to the party-giving parents, she might have needlessly cost her child a friendship and shown Maddie that she was prone to flying off the handle. Had I scolded the kids in the car for their callous remarks about Jeffrey and reported them to their parents, I might never have been in the position to help them reach a practical solution.

You want your child to know that you're available and reliable—and that asking for help is always an option when your child faces a problem, big or small. But it's only through your patient encouragement to solve problems when the stakes are low—as they are in these examples—that he'll learn where the limits of his own abilities lie. He'll know the difference between small problems, like a bratty kid who hogs the swing, and big ones, like a bully intimidating younger children. He'll know when he can rely on himself and when he needs adult help.

If you teach your child to handle challenging situations independently when he's young and the problems are relatively small, the practice will help him cope effectively with bigger challenges later on. Ideally, few will be as dramatic as the one faced by seven Boston University students, who were so ill-practiced at self-reliance that, when their off-campus house caught fire, they called a parent to ask what to do, instead of dialing 911.[1] Yes, this really happened. It made the national news in 2012.

Early Decisions

Just as we reflexively leap in to shield our kids from challenges, we're naturally impelled to make decisions for them. In earlier chapters, we've discussed the age-appropriate responsibilities, in various realms of life, that we want to transfer to our children. Some of the "decisions" we want them to make are unconscious; others are to be made in full awareness. The Life's Work sidebar on page 214 recaps some of the important choices we want children to make independently, and the Reset sidebars in the relevant chapters suggest corrective actions parents can take to get kids on track.

As you can see from the Life's Work sidebar on page 214, practically every process that we've discussed in this book is aimed at teaching our kids to make good decisions independently. So, when we take control of these processes, or try impose certain behavior on our kids rather than elicit it, we're both depriving ourselves of the most effective means to achieve our parental goals and depriving our kids of essential practice in decision making; we're robbing them of self-reliance.

Of course, not all the choices that children have to make are momentous. As with problem solving, it's wise to get them in the habit of making decisions when the stakes are low. It pays to be conscious of times when there's no pressing need for adult involvement so we can step back and let kids decide things for themselves. Sometimes their decision making has unexpected benefits, as this story from my practice (and my own life) shows.

> Larry was planning to fly alone cross country with his two kids, four-and-half-year-old Robbie and three-year-old Lucy. "I'm really dreading it," he said, "but both our families live on the West Coast. Last year the flight was a nightmare when we did it with two adults. Even though there were TVs on the back of the seats, the kids got stir-crazy. And these days, other passengers tend to be nasty when kids get cranky."
>
> "You might be surprised this time," I told him. "Kids can be much better travelers than we expect. When mine get sick of being cooped up, I have them dig into their fun bags."
>
> "What are those?"
>
> "They're bags that the kids pack themselves with all the stuff they might want on the trip: books, stuffed

animals, puzzles and games, little toys, sketch pads and crayons, snacks—whatever they think they'll enjoy. I tell them to make sure that they bring along plenty of things they like because it's up to them to stay entertained."

"And they do it? Pack themselves?"

"Sure. I mean, it's not a perfect system—I do make a final check, make sure that what they've selected is appropriate, and offer reminders such as, 'Did you want to bring your teddy bear?' If the answer is yes, I have my child go get it. If something's inappropriate for a confined space, I have them pick something else.

"But when they've chosen what to bring, they seem to look forward to playing with it. You don't get that 'Mom, there nothing to do' argument. Or at least not as much. And if you do, you can say, 'But you picked your toys. You must have something you like to play with in there.'"

"What if they pack the whole playroom?"

I laughed. "Well, they're limited to what can fit in a wheeled backpack. If they bring too much and the bag is heavy, they'll know better the next time."

A week later, I got an email from Larry. It read, "Greetings from the Golden State. The fun bags saved the day."

Just like adults, children who make their own choices are far more likely to stand by them. If you pack up things you think they'll enjoy, there's too often room for argument: "But I don't like this book!" "I'm tired of that game." But when it's up to them, kids do identify the things that will keep them occupied. So you've solved two problems: you're spared the aggravation of packing, and the kids are more likely to stay amused. But most

continued on page 216

Life's Work

Effective parenting means that throughout our kids' childhood, we assign them progressively greater degrees of autonomy in order to help them become self-reliant. Here are some of the ways that we can let them take the lead in decision making and problem solving.

- **Sleep.** The most successful way to get children on a regular schedule is to create an environment conducive to sleep and to pay attention to when they get sleepy. Their natural drowsiness cycles can help them decide when to sleep. We can let them learn how to soothe themselves by not springing to attention at every whimper.

- **Comfort.** Self-soothing is a very important life skill. With your help, even very young children can discover and decide on preferred modes of self-soothing (such as using a pacifier or sucking their fingers, or choosing a safe age-appropriate alternative for a toddler like a favorite stuffed animal or a blanket), and that can help them become self-sufficient.

- **Meals.** We can promote self-feeding by allowing kids to select their own little utensils. We can help picky toddlers achieve a balanced diet by letting them choose from a broad range of healthy food choices. And we can encourage preschoolers and older children to expand their food horizons by letting them pick out items from the healthy food aisles at the supermarket, choose the condiments that will make less appealing foods palatable, and help pick out recipes that they want to help us make.

- **Elimination.** Toilet training is most effectively done by creating a conducive learning environment for potty training and then simply letting toddlers decide when they're ready to trade up from diapers, for daytime and nighttime.

- **Play.** Even infants can learn to problem solve. Seemingly simple, age-appropriate play can help develop an infant's motor skills. We can facilitate by placing interesting objects slightly out of reach and offering children toys that invite manipulation. We can give toddlers and preschoolers a range of play options, keeping toys on low shelves so they can decide on their own activities. When we play with them, we can foster problem-solving skills by letting them direct us, deciding on storylines and other imaginative elements. When they play on their own, we can also encourage creativity by letting them decide what to do or make (resisting their efforts to have us instruct them). In doing so, we teach them to be self-reliant, generating their own entertainment.

- **Discipline.** Rather than impose discipline, we can elicit desirable behavior by letting a child decide whether to observe limits and rules or else face reasonable consequences tailored to the "crime." Encouraging children to decide to behave well by letting them track their progress and rewarding them appropriately when they succeed makes discipline much less contentious and teaches important life skills.

- **Daily Responsibilities.** Kids should be encouraged to choose what to wear, to experiment with their own taste, to build their self-reliance. Ultimately, our goal should be to have our children learn basic responsibilities such as how to get themselves ready to go in the morning and how to pitch in around the house by giving them jobs they can make their own.

- **Conflict Resolution.** We can and should encourage kids to keep peace with siblings and friends by setting limits, guiding, and redirecting. It's our job to teach them to use words to assert themselves and settle disagreements, not by feeding them lines but by sparking them to decide what to say. Unless it's essential, we shouldn't intervene in conflicts but should allow kids to decide independently (within reason) how to resolve them. The recognition that they are not helpless but have the power to advocate for themselves is a major pillar of self-reliance.

continued from page 213

important, in a low-stakes situation, you've let children assume the responsibility for making decisions.

It's important not to be judgmental of every choice our children make. Whether or not we approve of some of those choices, we want them to have the confidence to attempt decisions. When we learn what they've decided, we can guide them—but not by saying something critical, like "Why on earth would you do that?" or "What made you think that was a good idea?"

If it's necessary to steer them toward better choices, we can spur them to think of alternatives, with questions like "What would be another way to handle a kid being mean to you?" or, in the case of the fun bags, "I'm really not so sure that the marshmallow gun is the best thing to use on the plane. What would be another fun toy to bring?"

When they manage to think up preferable options, we can praise them and explore how they'd go about implementing the better solution.

When they make good choices to begin with—and, with practice, they will—they deserve our praise even more.

Give and Take Recap

Here are some at-a-glance suggestions for helping pre-schoolers and kindergartners, in particular, make decisions and solve problems. The Life's Work sidebar on page 214 describes the often unconscious problem-solving and decision-making capabilities that, throughout this book, we've discussed eliciting from younger children.

- **Build Self-Reliance.** Help your children learn self-reliance by encouraging them to find solutions to their own problems. Before you step in to assist with their problems, pause, empathize, ask questions, be patient, and work with your child to find a solution.

- **Encourage Low-Stakes Problem Solving.** Wrestling with a low-stakes problem helps children develop valuable skills for solving the bigger problems they will face in the future.

- **Handling Disappointment.** Guiding your children through smaller disappointments will enable them to cope with larger disappointments yet to come.

CHAPTER 10

The Good Word: The Power of Appropriate Praise

Two preschool girls were talking in my office waiting room when I arrived. As I stopped to say hello, I heard one of them ask the other, "So, what do you get at soccer? Is it a trophy or a medal?"

I greeted the girl, adding, "Are you going to play soccer?"

"Maybe," she said.

Her mother and I exchanged a smile.

"Soccer is a lot of fun," I told her. "Kids really enjoy it."

"I hope I can get a medal," she replied.

Over the past few decades, it's become common to reward every single child who participates in an activity with some kind of prize, like a medal or a trophy. Some parents think prizes motivate kids and underscore that preschoolers are playing for fun, not for competition. Others think universal prizes trivialize true achievement and see them as part of an unhealthy cultural trend.

Certainly, the conversation in my waiting room suggests that prizes confuse some kids. Playing soccer offers children many great benefits: vigorous exercise, motor skill development, the experience of belonging to a team, cooperating with others, and so on. For kids under the age of six, the more free-form "swarm ball" or "beehive soccer," as it's called because it's so chaotic, can still be a lot of energy-burning fun. But when there's an award just for playing, rather than achieving something special, having fun is no longer the main goal. This raises a very important question: shouldn't having fun be more of reward in itself than a plastic medal?

On another note, in a humorous article on helicopter parenting in the Fort Worth, Texas, *Star-Telegram*, Barbara Rodriguez, the writer, confessed to photocopying e. e. cummings poems in the library to show a teacher the validity of her son's "creative" spelling.[1] As parents, we're likely to laugh at these stories, but with a grimace of recognition. After all, many parents have, at one time or another, been guilty of grade-grubbing for their kids—a double whammy of sparing them real-world judgment and preventing them from learning from their mistakes.

But teachers are in on the game, too. Studies by the well-known researchers Stuart Rojstaczer and Christopher Healy show that, today, 43 percent of the grades assigned in American four-year colleges are As, up from a mere 15 percent in 1960, with private schools being the biggest inflaters. The reason for the upswing is not that students are better prepared or working harder but rather that lenient graders get more favorable student reviews and seemingly give kids a competitive edge in academia and the job market. As a result of this grade inflation, it has grown harder for employers and graduate schools to tell the difference between excellent and merely competent (or worse) candidates.[2]

The culture of entitlement also has reached deeply into the workplace, with employers like Lands' End and Bank of America reportedly taking on consultants to teach managers to lavish praise and prizes on young hires. According to Bob Nelson, one such consultant quoted in the *Wall Street Journal*, young workers need near-constant feedback and like to be rewarded with "high-tech name-brand merchandise." He says, "It's not enough to give praise only when they're exceptional because for years they've been getting praise just for showing up."[3]

What's wrong with this trend? Stanford researcher and esteemed psychology professor Carol Dweck, who has been studying children and praise for decades, has long cautioned that kids lauded for everyday activities lose motivation, since there's nothing to strive for if you expect constant praise.[4] T. Berry Brazelton, the pediatrician and author hailed as "the most influential baby doctor since Doctor Spock," said in a *New York Times* interview that overpraised children grow dependent on external sources of approval, meaning that they don't develop "the inner motivation to challenge themselves."[5]

We know that, to succeed in all realms of life, including their relationships, our children must have the "inner motivation" to grow and "challenge themselves." How can we help them develop this independent drive and sense of pride in their competence? The answer lies not in the power of praise, but rather in *appropriate* praise.

Something for Nothing

While it's understandable why we might try to keep children's sports free of performance pressure, the fact of the matter is that kids are naturally competitive. Most preschool age—or even kindergarten—kids are not physically or emotionally ready for intense win/lose sports, but they're nevertheless goal-oriented. Think about it: In other activities, we continually encourage them to improve. We applaud them for learning to color within the lines, for mastering numbers and letters, for using their words effectively, for accomplishing all their chores, and so on. The pride they take in achieving improvements is a major source of self-esteem. It only stands to reason that they'd want a measure of progress on the playing field too.

That's why the everyone-gets-a medal practice doesn't ultimately do much to motivate or inspire children. There's no sense of mastery involved. In the short term, prizes might make kids happy, but it doesn't take long before they realize that such awards are meaningless because they're not connected to achievement. When everyone gets a medal, nobody wins.

> My friend Gillian and I spent the afternoon watching our kids play Little League baseball. As we headed back to the car, with the kids trailing behind, we passed a field where a tee ball game was breaking up. The kindergarten-age players were swarming the coaches.
>
> "Aren't they cute? Gillian said. "They're so excited about the game."
>
> "Adorable," I agreed.
>
> As we drew closer, we could hear what they were all saying: "Who won? Who won?"

"Isn't that weird?" Gillian asked. "I mean, they don't have outs in tee ball. They don't even keep score, do they?

"No," I said. "But I guess it's natural. They play their hearts out, so they figure that somebody had to win."

If your child's league gives medals to all participants, it wouldn't be reasonable to deprive your child of his. One way to handle it is to regard the medal simply as an acknowledgement that he is embarking on something new and trying his best. But when you talk to your child, what you'll want to emphasize is the process he's undertaking—the sport he's learning, what he likes about it, the skills that he feels he's developing, and so on. You want him to focus on the real gains he's making, which will persist long after the medal is forgotten.

The Praise Paradox

It may seem counterintuitive, but too much praise can rob kids of a sense of competence and undermine their self-esteem. Carol Dweck's studies, among others, highlight the fact that praising kids for being smart or talented can backfire. For example, in one study called "Parent Praise," Dweck and her colleagues observed parents with children who were fourteen to thirty-six months old, to see if they praised kids for personal qualities ("You're really smart," which is "person-based praise") or for the way they performed a task ("You tried hard," which is "process praise"). When the researchers revisited the same kids at ages seven and eight, they discovered that those given process praise were much more eager for challenges, believing that they could change for the better; while the ones praised for personal qualities were more averse to risk.[6]

Another Dweck study, this time with fifth graders, shows similar responses to the different kinds of praise emerging even in the short term. Two groups of kids were given easy tests. After the tests were scored, kids in one group were told that they'd done well because they were smart. The kids in the other group were told that they'd scored high because they'd tried hard.

Then both groups were given a second tougher test. The children in the "smart," or person-based praise, group protested, resisting the more difficult task. The kids in the "tried hard," or process-praise group, by contrast, welcomed the challenge.

Then the groups were given a third test, another easy one. The "smart" group found it rough going and scored lower than they had on the first easy test. The "tried hard" group not only scored even better than they had on the initial easy test, but actually outperformed the "smart" group. Apparently, the "smart" kids were daunted, even though the third test was easy, after their experience of being unable to breeze through the second test.[7]

Dweck has done many versions of this study, one of them with an interesting wrinkle. In that version, the researchers asked the kids to describe their scores to students in another school where the test would be administered. In the "smart" group, 40 percent of the subjects—unwilling to admit that they'd struggled—lied about their scores, compared to 10 to 12 percent of "tried hard" kids."[8]

As Dweck says, "People who believe in the power of talent tend not to fulfill their potential because they're so concerned with looking smart and not making mistakes. But people who believe that talent can be developed are the ones who really push, stretch, confront their own mistakes and learn from them."[9]

These studies are particularly relevant to what I hope to convey in this book about raising a self-reliant child, because it's almost automatic for parents today to shower children with the person-based "you're so smart" kind of praise. Once you start listening for it, you'll hear it constantly:

> "What a picture! You're such a good artist. Let's hang this on the refrigerator."
> "You're such a soccer star!"
> "You are a brilliant storyteller!"
> "You are the best reader!"
> "You're really gifted musically."

Chances are, you routinely express some of these sentiments yourself. While there are parents, I fear, who truly believe that they're raising little Picassos and Mozarts, Olympic athletes, and budding Nobel laureates (what a horrible burden to live with such over-the-top expectations!), most of us just toss off these remarks without thinking, eager to cheer on our children. Conventional wisdom over the past couple decades has held that praising children is essential to their self-esteem.

But the work of Dweck and others shows how debilitating this kind of "you're so great" praise can be. It leaves kids craving admiration—to the extent that they lie about test scores to supposed peers that they don't even know. They grow too anxious to apply themselves fully on a simple test because a hard one shook their confidence—and that's in front of researchers. Think how much more deeply invested children are in pleasing their parents.

If a child wins your approval for being a "good artist," being "great at soccer," being "brilliant," and so on, what happens when she's less than stellar? Does she even know what's made her "good," "great," or "brilliant"? She has no way to understand or to measure her achievement because what's being praised is, seemingly, a state of perfection.

This kind of praise is like candy, pleasing in the moment but not nourishing. It doesn't foster self-esteem any more than a sugar fix satisfies real hunger. Children come to crave such praise, especially in the absence of more sustaining fuel, but they eventually learn to distrust it. To feel that you're really proud of them, they need honest evaluations that they can believe in. They have to trust your praise for it to fuel their pride.

Persuasive Praise

It's perfectly natural for parents to want to praise their children for their accomplishments, but at the same time, we want our children to be motivated to succeed for themselves rather than for us as their parents.

> Two-and-a-half-year-old Tessa sat on the floor, happily assembling a puzzle, while her mother, Sheri, and I chatted in my office. It was a cute puzzle, made of wooden blocks shaped like a family of dogs that, when joined, were all snuggled together. Tessa was giggling as she made the pieces fit.
>
> "Mommy, look!" she would say as she connected the pieces. "The two baby dogs sleeping."
>
> "Why, Tessa," Sheri exclaimed. "You're so good with puzzles! I can hardly believe it."
>
> Sheri gave me a smile. A few minutes passed and then we heard, "Mommy! The babies and the daddy dog!"
>
> "That's really fantastic, honey," Sheri said. "You're so smart." Though her voice was animated, she rolled her eyes.

"That's Tessa's favorite puzzle," she told me in a half-whisper. "She plays with it constantly. She knows perfectly well how to put it together by now."

I must have looked surprised because Sheri asked, "Do you think that's odd? To keep doing the same puzzle over and over?"

"Not really," I assured her. "Kids love repetition."

"I'm so sick of going through the assembly with Tessa that I'm ready to throw it out," she replied.

Most parents are all too familiar with "repetition road." Toddlers, especially, love hearing the same stories and reading the same books again and again. The familiarity is comforting, and the repetition helps consolidate kids' developing language skills. As much as you may dread tucking into what seems like the thousandth iteration of *Good Night, Moon*, it can be warmly rewarding (not to mention beneficial) to have your child recite it right along with you.

But what Sheri was missing about the exchange was that it seemed to center on winning praise. While I'm sure that Tessa liked the cute nestling dogs, she was certainly angling for pats on the back from her mother. While it's great to be enthusiastic about what kids do, Sheri was going overboard. Tessa had already assembled the puzzle many times, so the surprise and delight that Sheri was expressing at her "skill" was disingenuous. By rolling her eyes, she even acknowledged that it was inauthentic.

It was also praise of the "you're-so-great" variety, which Dweck's "Parent Praise" study of toddlers correlated with fearing challenges when the children reached school age. Sheri certainly wasn't benefiting Tessa by stoking her with insincere and empty praise. Worse, she'd roused Tessa's expectations of receiving lots of attention and a virtual "sugar fix" of flattery when assembling the dog puzzle. Why would Tessa even try to move on to new and harder puzzles? She had a lot to lose by taking on something new that she might not assemble as easily and well.

It's very easy for such a dynamic to develop. Toddlers are learning so quickly and doing so many cute things that parents inevitably get excited. It can challenge their creativity to keep the praise meaningful and connected to the process. But slipping into the habit of slathering on the praise makes that praise untrustworthy.

That's why I always urge parents to soft-pedal the praise when their kids are young. Everything they do may fascinate you, but you have a lifetime of achievements to witness. So it pays to develop good habits and save the surprise and delight for genuine accomplishments. Your child's first steps are worthy of *oohs* and *ahhs*. So is the first time she spoons food into her mouth; the first time she dresses herself; the first sentence she utters; the first song she sings; the first time she draws letters and numbers, writes her name, or scrawls the words *Mommy* and *Daddy*.

Every scribble that she brings home from preschool, however, doesn't warrant the same breathless awe. Of course, you want to acknowledge those drawings, but much of the time, just saying aloud what your child has done, in a warm, loving voice, can be sufficient: "Oh, you made green and yellow lines." Or you can comment or ask questions about her choices: "That looks like glitter glue." "Tell me about this picture." "Did you cut out that pasted-on shape?"

Your interest is a powerful reward in itself. You don't need to pump it up with gushing, especially if the praise is out of sync with the achievement. Instead, develop a new reflex of taking a deep breath and pausing before you lay it on thick. Ask yourself, "What's the appropriate level of excitement for this accomplishment?"

You don't want to run out of adjectives before your child is out of diapers. But more than that, of course, you want your

Action Praise

Throughout this book, we've talked about praising children when they take the independent actions of, say, leaving the room when they want to use a pacifier, speaking up when they need the toilet or even getting there on their own, playing peacefully and creatively with others, mastering their emotions, getting themselves ready in the morning, using words instead of swatting a sibling, resolving problems effectively or kindly, and so on. When you think about an average day with your child, this can start to seem like quite an avalanche of praise. But it's less the sheer volume of praise that makes children approval dependent and risk averse than the way we express our approbation.

Here are some suggestions for delivering appropriate praise to children old enough to understand, like older toddlers and preschoolers.

- **Staying in Own Bed.** "I can see that you've really been trying to stay in your own bed. I'm glad that you seem to be growing comfortable there, like a big kid.

- **Self-Soothing.** "You seem to enjoy being with the family rather than going into your room with your pacifier. It's fine when you leave, but we love having you with us too." Also, "You've been thinking of really good ways get to sleep without your pacifier."

- **Self-Feeding and Trying New Foods.** "You took a mighty mouthful of peas! I bet you can do it with the squash, too." "Let's see if you can bite off the leaves of the [broccoli] tree."

child to be independently engaged in her own process of discovery and creation rather than become a "praise junkie," pumped up by the prospect of your ecstatic fussing.

- **Toilet Training.** "Thank you for telling me you needed the potty." "Hooray—you get to mark the chart."

- **Active Play.** "I love seeing the pictures you draw." "I enjoyed being the dragon in our game." "The princess in our game had such interesting adventures." "You and your friend are taking turns with the cars so well."

- **Tantrum Control and Discipline.** "It's fun to have you help pick out things in the supermarket." "We're having lunch together in the restaurant just like grownups." "You're getting better and better at using your words."

- **Daily Responsibilities.** "You picked out such an interesting combination of colors and patterns when you got dressed all by yourself this morning." "We got in a good walk together." "Thank you for bringing in the newspaper." "I really appreciate the way you pick up your toys." "Wow, all your dirty clothes are in the hamper." "You put on your pajamas in record time." "It's such a big help when you put away the silverware."

- **Conflict Resolution.** "I loved hearing you sing to the new baby." "It's such a help when you hand me the baby's diaper." "Thank you for letting your brother use the red crayon." "You shared nicely with your friend." "You're using your words so well." "What a good idea you had to solve the problem." "I think you had a good insight about why your friend was crying."

- **Problem Solving and Decision Making.** "What a good idea you had for fixing that." "I really like the solution you came up with."

An important note: When you do praise your child, be descriptive. Avoid the "you're-so-great," sugar-fix kind of praise and compliment the action rather than the person. That way, you give your child a concrete thought to retain and build on. You can say (if true):

"You used some new color combinations in this picture."
"It looked fun when you went down the slide."
"The other team could hardly catch you on the soccer field."
"I like the way the people talk in your story."
"You sound like you enjoy reading aloud."
"You worked really hard on your math problems."
"I can tell you've been practicing the piano."

The Action Praise sidebar on page 228 offers more suggestions for formulating words of praise in the areas that we've covered in this book. If you keep your praise low-key, descriptive, and sincere, you'll become a reliable critic for your child. You'll give your child something real to be proud of—a sense of achievement and competence that is the foundation of self-esteem.

The Fail Factor

Pride and a sense of competence are major factors in self-esteem, but T. Berry Brazelton adds another. In his view—one that I share—healthy self-esteem "allows a child to confront her mistakes without taking apart her positive feelings about herself, so that she can mobilize these positive feelings . . . to find the courage to learn from her mistakes."[10]

How can we help our kids accept and learn from the mistakes that they'll inevitably make? First of all, we help by not overreacting, by keeping the child's disappointment the primary focus rather than any feelings of our own. We can also help by modeling how to cope with disappointments, big and small. Our children don't yet have our sense of proportion and often don't distinguish between inconsequential errors and ones that matter more. And they often don't know how to begin to process a mistake in their minds.

Among other things, this means that it's beneficial for kids to hear us talk through mistakes and disappointments, showing that we don't allow them to defeat us and highlighting what we've learned. For example:

> Today I made a silly mistake. I decided that since the weather was so nice, I'd ride my bike to the store. I put on my helmet, stuck a bottle of water in the basket, and then I hit the road. But wouldn't you know it, after I rode all the way there, I realized that I'd forgotten the lock. I could just picture it, hanging there in the garage.
>
> I couldn't leave the bike unlocked and go shopping, so I had to turn around and come back home. Oh, well, at least I had a nice ride in the sunshine. But now I'll definitely remember to bring the lock with me next time.

Here's another example:

> Today my tennis partner and I played a game of tennis against two other players. We'd watched them play before, and we felt pretty sure that we could win. But they played really well today. The game was close, and then I kept double faulting on my serve. They ended up winning 6–4. My partner was disappointed, and I felt bad. I told her I was sorry that the ball got away from me. Next time, I'll try to concentrate harder. Sometimes you win; sometimes you lose. We'll play those two again, and maybe next time, we'll be the winners.

This kind of modeling gives children sample scripts, which they can adapt for their own challenging situations. When doing this kind of modeling, it's best to resist the self-deprecation that we often fall into when relating such stories to a friend, like saying, "I'm such a dope!" or "What an idiot I am!"

Young children don't always grasp that this kind of negative talk is exaggerated and a form of humor. It sends them a message that we want to avoid, which is like the equally discouraging negative version of person-based, "you're-so-great" type praise—again, judging the person, not the action.

What we want to convey is that mistakes and disappointments are a natural part of life. They teach us lessons—to be

Praise Reset

Does your child show you every line she draws, just so you'll say, "How beautiful"? Does she say, "Look at me! Watch me!" every time she throws a ball? All children love to have their parents watch and comment on what they do, but if such requests are constant, chances are you've gone a bit overboard in your praise. Children can become praise addicts, which impairs their development of true self-esteem.

So it's wise to regroup and begin to get your praise on a more realistic footing. Beginning to wean your child off excessive praise may require some self-examination and self-restraint.

- **Pause before you praise** and ask honestly how much attention the achievement really deserves.

- **Make neutral comments for minor achievements,** like "Interesting," "It looks like you're starting a picture," or "It seems that you like to pitch."

sure to bring the lock, to stay focused on the game. When we disappoint others, like the tennis partner, we apologize. The next time we're in a similar situation, we remember our mistake and try harder so that it doesn't happen again.

It's also good to tell your child explicitly that making mistakes—even screwing up in major way—does nothing to undermine your love for him. I often find myself saying to my own kids, in cases of carelessness, "I know that's not how you usually like to do things. Today was a bad day." Or, in cases of misbehavior, "That didn't feel like you, to me. I know that you usually listen to what I say, and that this was an exception."

- **When you do praise, stop gushing.** Stay measured and focused on the process. You can say: "What colors are you planning to add next?" "Tell me why you chose those colors." "Who's your favorite person to play catch with?" or "Do you like kicking the ball as much as throwing?"

- **Avoid person-based, "you're so great" sort of praise.** If you can't think of a way to comment on the process itself, you can comment on the potential outcome or the general circumstances of the activity. You can say, "It will be fun to see how that picture turns out" or "I'm glad to see you having fun throwing."

- **If your child still keeps fishing for praise,** you can say, "You know what I really enjoy? Seeing you learn so many new things."

When it comes to more process-related mistakes, I think that it's vitally important for kids to understand that we all have to work for things. Not everyone is going to be instantly successful at every activity. Nobody gets 100 percent on every test, in school or in life.

Yes, for some of us, certain successes come easily, but most things we try stand a good chance of being hard at the outset. Learning is a process, and achievement doesn't mean quick triumph but trying hard and improving over time. True self-esteem comes from improving—and even from recovering when we fail.

An Inner Journey

The reason that I like martial arts so much as an activity for children, and why I believe so many kids really blossom in the practice, is that martial arts students progress in well-defined steps through levels of competence at their own pace. They begin with the white belt, which stands for courage—the courage to try something new. Then, two or three times a week, for months or even years, they go through pretty much the same repertoire of movements, getting better and better with each class. Kids don't get bored by the repetition, because they feel themselves improving.

They're guided by observation and by the example of higher-ranked students, who stand in front of them. They're all repeating the same exercises, and as they grow more accomplished, they earn a succession of new belts, which they wear with pride.

My daughter started in martial arts when she was six years old, and at nine, she achieved her black belt. That thrills me, and more importantly, it makes her proud. She didn't stick with martial arts to please her parents, but for her own satisfaction and sense of mastery. And now she's achieved a very significant milestone.

Each belt she earned along the way reflects a step on her journey toward mastery of the practice. Isn't that the perfect way to characterize a child's growing independence on the path to adulthood? A personal journey toward mastery—toward self-reliance. For each child, the journey unfolds at a unique pace. Our most sacred job as parents is guiding our children on the paths they choose, when they are ready to take them.

The Good Word Recap

Here are some guidelines for offering appropriate praise— the kind that fuels rather than undermines self-esteem— for children at various ages. The Action Praise sidebar on page 228 offers examples of appropriate praise for each of the subject areas we've explored in this book.

- **One to Three Years.** Praise the way children *do* things ("process praise"), not their personal qualities ("person-based" praise).

- **Three Years On.** Teach your children how to handle their mistakes rather than be devastated by them. Share your own mistakes and disappointments to give them a "script" for dealing with their own: describe the mistake, why you made it, what you learned from it, how you made up for it, and how you forgave yourself and let it go. When you child makes a mistake, assure him of your love but don't gloss over the mistake.

Notes

Introduction

1. Jennifer Ludden, "Helicopter Parents Hover in the Workplace," National Public Radio, *All Things Considered*, February 6, 2012.
2. Lenore Skenazy, "America's Worst Mom?" *New York Sun*, April 8, 2008.
3. Lenore Skenazy, *Free-Range Kids: Giving Our Children the Freedom We Had Without Going Nuts with Worry* (Hoboken, NJ: Jossey-Bass, 2010).
4. Amy Chua, "Why Chinese Mothers Are Superior," *Wall Street Journal*, January 8, 2011.
5. Lisa Belkin, "Calling Mom a Hippo," *New York Times*, April 27, 2011.
6. Elaine Sciolino, "Maman Knows Best," *New York Times*, February 24, 2010.
7. Sandra Ammodt, PhD, and Sam Wang, PhD, *Welcome to Your Child's Brain: How the Mind Grows from Conception to College* (New York: Bloomsbury USA, 2011).
8. Sandra Ammodt, PhD, and Sam Wang, PhD, "Building Self-Control, the American Way," *New York Times*, February 17, 2012.
9. "Surprising Facts About Birth in the United States," August 2011, www.babycenter.com/0_surprising-facts-about-birth-in-the-united-states_1372273.bc.

10. Ibid.

11. Tara Parker-Pope, "Surprisingly, Family Time Has Grown," *New York Times*, April 5, 2010.

Chapter 1

1. Marc Weissbuth, MD, *Healthy Sleep Habits, Happy Child* (New York: Random House, 2009): 18.

2. Julie Deardorff (moderator), "Babies' Sleeping Issues: Live Health Chat," *Chicago Tribune*, March 15, 2011.

3. Louise S. Foley, Ralph Maddison, Yannan Jiang, Samantha Marsh, Timothy Olds, and Kate Ridley, "Presleep Activities and Time of Sleep Onset in Children," *Pediatrics* 131, no. 2 (February 1, 2013): 276–282.

4. Evelyne Touchette, BSc, Dominique Petit, PhD, Jan Paquet, PhD, Michel Boivin, PhD, Chista Japel, PhD, Richard E. Tremblay, PhD, and Jacques Y. Montplaisir, MD, PhD, "Factors Associated with Fragmented Sleep at Night Across Early Childhood," *Archives of Pediatrics & Adolescent Medicine* 159, no. 3 (March 2005): 245.

5. Marc Weissbuth, MD, *Healthy Sleep Habits, Happy Child* (New York: Random House, 2009).

6. Ibid., 198, 207.

7. Deardorff, "Babies' Sleeping Issues."

8. Richard Ferber, MD, *Solve Your Child's Sleep Problems* (New York: Touchstone, 2006), 62.

9. Ibid., 71.

10. Touchette et al., "Factors Associated with Fragmented Sleep," 242–249.

11. Ferber, *Child's Sleep Problems*, 49.

12. American Academy of Pediatrics Task Force on Sudden Infant Death Syndrome, 2005–2006, "The Changing Concept of Sudden Infant Death Syndrome: Diagnostic Coding Shifts, Controversies Regarding the Sleeping Environment, and New Variables to Consider in Reducing Risk," *Pediatrics* 116, no. 5 (November 2005): 1247.

13. American Academy of Pediatrics Task Force on Sudden Infant Death Syndrome, "SIDS and Other Sleep-Related Infant Deaths: Expansion of Recommendations for a Safe Infant Sleeping Environment," *Pediatrics* 128, no. 5 (November 2011): e1341–67.
14. American Academy of Pediatrics Task Force, "Sudden Infant Death Syndrome," 1245–1246.
15. US Consumer Product Safety Commission, "Safer Cribs for Babies Available Starting Today," Release #11–260 (June 28, 2011).
16. Ibid.

Chapter 2

1. American Academy of Pediatrics, "Pacifiers: Satisfying Your Baby's Needs," last modified May 12, 2011, www.healthychildren.org.

Chapter 3

1. American Academy of Pediatrics, "Switching to Solid Food," last modified February 27, 2012, www.healthychildren.org.
2. Deanna A. Stephens, "Winning the Food Fights," last modified May 1, 2012, www.healthychildren.org.
3. American Academy of Pediatrics, "AAP Reaffirms Breastfeeding Guidelines," last modified February 26, 2012, www.healthy children.org.

Chapter 4

1. Nathan Blum, MD, Bruce Taubman, MD, and Nicole Nemeth, MD, "Relationship Between Age at Initiation of Toilet Training and Duration of Training: A Prospective Study," *Pediatrics* 111, no. 4 (April 1, 2003): 810–814.
2. American Academy of Pediatrics, "How to Tell When Your Child Is Ready," last modified January 12, 2012, www.healthychildren.org.

3. American Academy of Pediatrics, "Stages of Toilet Training: Different Skills, Different Schedules," last modified November 30, 2010, www.healthychildren.org.

Chapter 5

1. American Academy of Pediatrics Policy Statement, "Media Use by Children Younger than Two Years," *Pediatrics* 128, no. 5 (November 1, 2011): 1040.
2. Gwenn Schurgin O'Keeffe, MD, "Pediatrics Now: Overview— New Media," *Pediatric Clinics of North America* 59, no. 3 (June 2012): 595.
3. Kate Zernicke, "Fast Tracking to Kindergarten?" *New York Times*, May 13, 2011.
4. American Academy of Pediatrics Policy Statement, "Media Use by Children Younger than Two Years," *Pediatrics* 128, no. 5 (November 1, 2011): 1043.
5. Ibid., 1042.
6. Ibid.
7. Ibid.
8. American Academy of Pediatrics, "Increasing Physical Activity during Preschool Years," last modified July 30, 2012, www.healthychildren.org.
9. Deanna A. Stephens, "Caution: Children at Play," last modified May 2, 2012, www.healthychildren.org.

Chapter 6

1. Alison Bath, "Despite Opposition, Paddling Students Allowed in Nineteen States," *USA Today*, April 23, 2012.
2. Brendan L. Smith, "The Case Against Spanking," American Psychological Association *Monitor on Psychology* 43, no. 4 (April 2012): 60.
3. Ibid.

Chapter 7

1. Elizabeth Kolbert, "Spoiled Rotten: Why Do Kids Rule the Roost?" *New Yorker*, July 2, 2012, www.newyorker.com/arts/critics/books/2012/07/02/120702crbo_books_kolbert.
2. Rebecca A. Clay, "Helping Kids Care," American Psychological Association, *Monitor on Psychology* 37, no. 11 (December 2006): 42.

Chapter 9

1. Lisa Belkin, "Dorm on Fire? Who You Shouldn't Call First," *Huffington Post*, January 24, 2012.

Chapter 10

1. Barbara Rodriguez, "Take Hover from Being a Helicopter Parent," *Dallas Fort-Worth Star-Telegram*, October 6, 2011.
2. Catherine Rampell, "Grade Inflation: Your Questions Answered," *New York Times*, May 13, 2010.
3. Jeffrey Zaslow, "The Most Praised Generation Goes to Work," *Wall Street Journal*, April 20, 2007.
4. Janet Rae-Dupree, "If You're Open to Growth, You Tend to Grow," *New York Times*, July 6, 2008.
5. Tara Parker-Pope, "T. Berry Brazelton on Self-Esteem, Discipline, and Learning from Your Kids," *New York Times*, September 14, 2008.
6. Jenny Anderson, "Too Much Praise Is No Good for Toddlers," *New York Times*, October 27, 2011.
7. Ibid.
8. Alina Tugend, "The Many Errors in Thinking About Mistakes," *New York Times*, November 24, 2007.
9. Rae-Dupree, "If You're Open to Growth, You Tend to Grow."
10. Parker-Pope, "T. Berry Brazelton on Self-Esteem, Discipline, and Learning from Your Kids."

About the Author

Dr. Alanna Levine is a practicing pediatrician in New York and the mother of two school-age children. Dr. Levine joined Orangetown Pediatric Associates in 2002 and is also on staff at Englewood Hospital and Medical Center in New Jersey. She is passionate about delivering accurate health messages to parents and accomplishes this through national media appearances on Fox News Channel, CBS, NBC, and ABC. She has also been quoted in numerous publications such as *Parents* magazine, *New York Magazine*, and *USA Today*.

Dr. Levine is a spokesperson for the American Academy of Pediatrics and is on the Executive Committee for their Council on Communications and Media. She is also a Clinical Assistant Professor of Pediatrics at New York Medical College.

Prior to joining Orangetown Pediatric Associates, Dr. Levine completed her internship and residency at Mount Sinai Hospital in New York City. She obtained her medical degree from the Sackler School of Medicine in Tel Aviv, Israel, and a master's in Medical Sciences from Boston University. She completed her undergraduate education at the University of Wisconsin with a major in Psychology. Visit www.alannalevinemd.com.

Index

everyone-gets-a medal,
218–19, 221–22
guidelines, age-
based, 235
inner journey and,
234–35
learning from mistakes
and, 230–34
overview, 218–220
person-based versus
process-based,
222–25, 233
persuasive, 225–230
reset for, 232–33
Preschoolers
boundaries for
acceptable
behavior, 185
decision making
and problem
solving, 217
introducing conflict
resolution, 178
mealtime, 83–89
playtime, 124–130
sleep, 43–45
Prizes and rewards,
103–4, 218–19,
221–22
Problem solving
broken toys and,
196–99
decisions, kids making,
211–17
letting kids take the
lead in, 199–202,
209–11, 214–15
overview, 217
praise appropriate f
or, 229
reset for, 206–7
in social activities,
202–11
talk throughs for,
141–42
toilet training and, 101

See also Conflict
resolution
Pull-ups (training pants),
97, 104–5, 110

Reading, or being read
to, 125
Redirection, 178, 193
Responsibilities. *See*
Tasks and
responsibilities
Rewards and prizes,
103–4, 218–19,
221–22

Safety issues
bottle feeding, 66–67
button batteries, 198
honey, 74, 91
pacifiers, 57–58
sleep, 34–35
for starting solid foods,
74–75
sudden infant death
syndrome (SIDS),
32, 34, 49
toys in bed, 41
Sears, William, 3
Self-esteem
boosting, 166
foundation of, 230
handling mistakes
and, 234
source of, 221
too much praise and,
222, 224
Self-feeding
babies interest in,
73–76
encouraging, 214, 228
recommendations on,
77–78, 91
Self-soothing
finger-sucking, 60–62
guidelines, by age,
62–63

learning, 21, 214
praise appropriate
for, 228
See also Pacifiers
Sharing, 186–89, 205–6
Sherpa parents, 154
Shopping for groceries,
with kids, 87, 140
Sibling rivalry. *See*
Conflict resolution
SIDS (sudden infant
death syndrome),
32, 34, 49
Sippy cup, 68, 69–71,
77, 91
Skenazy, Lenore, 4–5
Sleep
co-sleeping vs. bed
sharing, 32
Ferber Method, 28–32
first-year challenges,
23–24
getting back on track,
32–37
importance of, 19–20
independent, 39–40
learning to sleep, 8,
21–23, 214
naps, 20–21, 39
nighttime, 20–21, 26
positions for, 35
preschoolers, 43–45
rehearsal/calming rou-
tine, 26–27, 35, 36
reset for, 40–41
safety issues, 34–35
strategies for, by age,
46–47
television's effect on,
119–120
toddlers, 37–42,
46–47
Weissbluth Method,
24–28
Smoking, 35